# LIVING LOVE

# LIVING LOVE

## STUART & JILL BRISCOE

Harold Shaw Publishers
Wheaton, Illinois

ISBN 0-87788-488-9

Cover design by David LaPlaca

Cover photo © 1993 by Robert McKendrick

**Library of Congress Cataloging-in-Publication Data**

Briscoe, D. Stuart.
    Living love : what can happen when we learn to love God's
way / Stuart & Jill Briscoe.
        p.   cm.
    ISBN 0-87788-488-9
    1. Agape.   2. God—Love.   3. God—Worship and love.
    4. Spiritual life—Christianity.   I. Briscoe, Jill.   II. Title.
    BV4639.B815   1993
248.4—dc20                                              93-19608
                                                           CIP

99  98  97  96  95  94  93

10  9  8  7  6  5  4  3  2  1

# Contents

## Part 1
## The Basics of Love

# Part 2
## The Qualities of Love

# Part 3
# The Impact of Love

# The Basics of Love

"We begin at the real beginning, with love as the Divine energy. This primal love is Gift-love. In God there is no hunger that needs to be filled, only plenteousness that desires to give. . . . Divine Gift-love in the man enables him to love what is not naturally lovable; lepers, criminals, enemies, morons, the sulky, the superior, and the sneering. Finally, by a high paradox, God enables men to have a Gift-love toward Himself. There is, of course, a sense in which no one can give to God anything which is not already His; and if it is already His, what have you given? But since it is only too obvious that we can withhold ourselves, our wills and hearts, from God, we can, in that sense, also give them."

—C. S. *Lewis*, The Joyful Christian

# How do I say I love you?

I have loved you with an everlasting love; I have
drawn you with loving-kindness.        —*Jeremiah 31:3*

We're not always certain about the meaning of the word *love*.
I might say, "I love my wife. I love my dog." But you would
probably guess that the love I have for my wife is significantly
different from the love I have for my dog—and you would
be right. I feel about my wife the way a man should feel about
his wife, and I treat her in a way that indicates the way I feel
about her. Although I'm fond of the dog, I deal with him
another way entirely.

We use the word *love* all the time to cover a whole range of
feelings and actions. This can easily lead to misunderstandings.

Recently I was in an airport store where they had a collec-
tion of plaques called "Love is . . ." One said, "Love is a warm
puppy." Isn't that sweet? The next said, "Love is an itch you
cannot scratch." A bit of humor there. Another said, "Love is
never having to say you're sorry." Sounds profound.

But take those ideas and insert them into Scripture—"The
fruit of the Spirit is a warm puppy," "The fruit of the Spirit is
an itch you cannot scratch," "The fruit of the Spirit is never
having to say you're sorry"—and the meanings become ridiculous. So we need to be careful to distinguish between the biblical
meaning of "love" and the way it is commonly understood.

If we're not careful, nonbiblical ideas about love will affect
our spiritual lives. When our children were younger I listened
to some of the music they listened to. The words of one song
were: "How did we fall in lo-ove? How did we get in a mess
like this? What are we going to tell our friends?" Beautiful
lyrics, aren't they? I thought, *Does this really help me understand
what love is? Love is something you fall in. When you fall in it, it's*

*a mess. And when you fall in it, you're so embarrassed that you don't tell your friends.* When we're constantly exposed to re-definitions of love like these, it's no wonder we are confused about the biblical concept of love.

The English get a lot of mileage from the word *love*. People say, "I love strawberries. I love big hats. I love high winds. I love sunbathing. I love big dogs. I love French fries. I love cups of tea. I love the BBC." Often we say "I love" when we really mean, "I like." We use these two words interchangeably, as though their meanings were the same.

In the King James Bible (published in 1611), the word used for love is *charity*: "the greatest of these is charity." In our day giving to the church or giving to the poor is what most people think of when they hear that word. That's because the meaning of *charity* has changed dramatically from the meaning it had in the seventeenth century. At that time, the word did not convey giving a nickel to the United Way or digging into your pocket when the Salvation Army came along. *Charity* was an appropriate translation for *agape*, the love of God himself. So if the old word *charity* doesn't convey *agape* and the modern usage of *love* is not much better, we need to exercise greater care.

What is this *agape*, this very love of God? And how is it different from all the loves we know in our lives? More importantly, what does *agape* have to do with us?

As we will see, *agape* has *everything* to do with us. It is the love God has lavished upon us. And if we allow it, it is the love that can reshape every aspect of our lives.

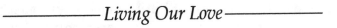 *Living Our Love*

Make a list of all the qualities of love you can think of. Which qualities seem impossible to maintain? Which do you want most in your life?

# Love cannot exclude God

> Dear friends, let us love one another, for love comes
> from God. Everyone who loves has been born of
> God and knows God. Whoever does not love does
> not know God, because God is love.     —*1 John 4:7-8*

Love is the essence of God's being—that's the first important
thing to know about love. There is nothing about God that is
not an expression of love.

Whatever we do, we must not exclude God from our
definition of love, because to do that would automatically
make it an inadequate definition. And we must be very
discerning about most of what has been written and por-
trayed by our contemporary society about love. The love it
projects has one very serious deficiency: it is so often wholly
unrelated to any concept of God.

The Bible states without apology: "God is love." If we want
to have any understanding of love at all, we must understand
that it has its roots, its origins, and its clearest demonstration
*in God himself.* There is no way that anybody can understand
love adequately without being able to some degree to understand God.

The mistake we often make is in trying so hard to understand *ourselves,* without understanding God. We think that if
we study human nature long enough, learn enough about
genetics and psychology and social dynamics, that we will in
fact discover the key to loving. But if we look only to ourselves
we are horribly limited. If we are to discover the true meaning

of love, we must discover God, our Creator, and the One who loves us.

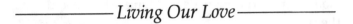
## Living Our Love

Spend some time in prayer and meditation asking these questions: What have I assumed to be true about love because of my family background? What has my culture taught me about love? In what way does my knowledge of God help me to understand love?

# God's love explained

> God created man in his own image, in the image of
> God he created him; male and female he created
> them.
> —*Genesis 1:27*

The apostle Paul, who evidently saw the need to explain the mysteries of God to relatively new Christians, gives us one effective picture of God's love in Romans 5:5-8:

> God has poured out his love into our hearts by the
> Holy Spirit, whom he has given us. You see, just at
> the right time, when we were still powerless, Christ
> died for the ungodly. Very rarely will anyone die
> for a righteous man, though for a good man some-
> one might possibly dare to die. But God demon-
> strates his own love for us in this: While we were
> still sinners, Christ died for us.

Two expressions in this passage stand out. In verse 5, Paul writes, "God has poured out his love into our hearts," and in verse 8: "God demonstrates his own love for us in this: While we were still sinners, Christ died for us." This is one of the delightful passages of Scripture that actually takes time out to explain God's love to us.

Paul spends quite a lot of time explaining the human condition. And he paints a black backdrop against which he can project the brilliance of the love of God. Over and over, he explains that it was while we were in a very wretched condition that God loved us. We're sinners (verse 8); we're powerless (verse 6); we're ungodly (verse 6); and we're ene-mies (verse 10). He isn't trying to rub our noses in the dirt;

rather, he's trying to show us the wonder of the love of God being expressed to people who are so unworthy of it.

Paul goes on to explain that Christ died for sinners, and he makes the great statement stand out by contrasting how people's attitudes toward dying for others compares to Christ's. He says it's unlikely that anyone would die for a righteous man, though it is just possible that someone might dare to die for a good man. But the whole point is that we're not righteous and we're not good! We're sinners. Yet Christ died for sinners—those who are not righteous and not good. This begins to demonstrate the sheer immensity of the love of God. There are some people who actually really believe they are righteous. Some are convinced that they are good enough. But it doesn't take much observation—of the world in general or of our own hearts in particular—to agree with the Scripture that says, "there's none righteous" and there are none who make a habit of being or doing good.

We were created to bear the divine image and glory of God, as the verse in Genesis describes, but we lost it all through sin. We lack; we come short. The wonderful news of the love of God is that he loved us in that condition!

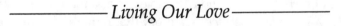

## Living Our Love

Imagine that you have never heard of God's existence. Imagine that never in your life have you heard or read the words, "God loves you." How would life be different?

# The Father loved the Son

> When all the people were being baptized, Jesus was
> baptized too. And as he was praying, heaven was
> opened and the Holy Spirit descended on him in
> bodily form like a dove. And a voice came from
> heaven: "You are my Son, whom I love; with you I
> am well pleased." —*Luke 3:21-22*

Do you ever think much about the fact that God loved Jesus? This is essential to our understanding of God's love.

From what Scripture says, it appears that Jesus was actually the first object of God's love. The Son is the original and the eternal object of the Father's love. Jesus Christ was with God in eternity living in conscious enjoyment of the love of God. "In the beginning was the Word, and the Word was with God, and the Word was God. He was with God in the beginning. Through him all things were made; without him nothing was made that has been made. . . . The Word became flesh and made his dwelling among us. We have seen his glory, the glory of the One and Only, who came from the Father" (John 1:1-3, 14). But he left heaven and came to earth as a man. There was a glory about the man Jesus, a glory that reminded people of God—legitimately, because he *was* God, the Word who was with God in the beginning. And God has an eternal affection for Jesus Christ, his Son. He existed long before Bethlehem, was loved by the Father, and walked the dusty lanes and hills of Galilee still enjoying that love. And as he approached the awesome cross he leaned on the Father's love, praying in the upper room, "Father, I want those you have given me to be with me where I am, and to see my glory, the glory you have given me because *you loved me before the creation of the world*" (John 17:24, italics added).

This eternal relationship reminds us that Jesus was a member of the Trinity. He was loved as a member of the eternal "family." But God had other reasons to love him. First of all, Jesus kept the first and second commandments: first, to love God with all your heart, soul, mind, and strength, and secondly, to love your neighbor as yourself. At Gethsemane Jesus was concerned with the Father's name, the Father's will, the Father's kingdom: "Not my will, but yours be done" (Luke 22:42). Jesus gave God his affectionate, undivided attention and devotion.

Also, God had reason to love Jesus because he offered himself—actually became a person, lived, died, and faced hell itself—so that God could gain back the creation he had lost: us.

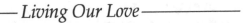

## Living Our Love

Think about Jesus' life and in what ways he acted as though he were in God's "family." What did he do and say that indicated he was confident of God's fatherly love?

# God loves those who love his Son

Remember that at that time you were separate from Christ, excluded from citizenship in Israel and foreigners to the covenants of the promise, without hope and without God in the world. But now in Christ Jesus you who once were far away have been brought near through the blood of Christ.

—*Ephesians 2:12-13*

Jesus is the eternal object of God's love. It follows, then, that God would hold a special place in his heart for those who love Christ. God's love, in a special way, is demonstrated to his family. I love my family in a way that is different from the way I love my friends or those I teach. And God's love for the believer in his family is evident from the Scriptures.

In John 14:21 Jesus says, "He who loves me will be loved by my Father." Do you love Jesus? If you do, Jesus promised you that you shall be loved by the Father. John 16:27 says, "The Father himself loves you because you have loved me and have believed that I came from God." God loves the believers because they believe that Jesus was divine. Do you believe? Then God loves you for that, too! Be glad you can know that you're loved.

And here's the best news of all: God the Father loves you as much as he loves Jesus Christ, his Son! And Jesus wanted the world to know: "May they be brought to complete unity to let the world know that you sent me and have loved them even as you have loved me" (John 17:23).

Do you feel loved by God? Look at some of the ways God loved Jesus, and you'll see how God loves you. Isaiah 42:1 expresses his delight in loving Jesus: "Here is my servant, whom I uphold, my chosen one in whom I delight." And he loves you as much as he loves Jesus. He delights in you because you've accepted his Son. You're in Christ if Christ is in you. You've been placed in his body, the church, of which Christ is the head. God looks at you and sees you in Christ, his Son.

In a sense, Jesus and God are the same; there is only one God whom we must worship. But in another sense, we are able to experience God in three distinct ways—through Father, Son, and Holy Spirit. What does this mean? It means that love comes to us from God in a variety of expressions. We can know God's king/parent love. We can know the brother/fellow human being love of Jesus, who understands our needs and concerns precisely, and we can know the counselor/comforter love of the Holy Spirit who dwells within us. We are able to be loved in all these ways because, in Jesus Christ, we have become the *family* of God.

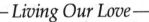

## Living Our Love

How do you feel when a family member is afraid, in pain, weary, angry, surprised, happy, relieved, worried? Which of these conditions best describes you right now? Spend some time in prayer, meditating on the fact that God feels even more intense empathy and care toward you than you feel toward your own family members.

# God's choice to love

> The LORD did not set his affection on you and
> choose you because you were more numerous than
> other peoples, for you were the fewest of all
> peoples. But it was because the LORD loved you and
> kept the oath he swore to your forefathers.
>
> —*Deuteronomy 7:7-8*

We know that God loves Jesus, and that he loves those who love his Son. But that brings up the question of the world *before* Jesus; did the ancient peoples know God's love?

As we read the Old Testament, we see that people at that time did become aware of God's love. He demonstrated his care to them through miracles, such as the Israelites' escape from Egypt and their incredible survival in the wilderness all those years. And he demonstrated his love through the laws he gave the people so that their lives would have order and peace (as long as they followed those laws, of course). But why did God love them? The Scripture passage cited above tells us plainly: he loved them because he chose to love them. Once God had made a promise to Abraham, generations earlier: "I will make you into a great nation and I will bless you" (Genesis 12:2). And God keeps his promises.

But God's love extended beyond Israel. Peter didn't think so. He thought God only loved Jews and rejected Gentiles until God gave him a vision and said, in essence, "Don't call unacceptable what I have accepted." Israel was simply the vehicle to produce the Messiah and to be the missionaries to the world. For God had *also* promised father Abraham, "All peoples on earth will be blessed through you" (Genesis 12:3).

So we see, first of all, that God chose to love Abraham and all his descendants—before anyone had even heard of Jesus.

And God continues to choose to love the whole world. It was his choice, dictated only by God's character, and not by anything any human being had ever done.

Have you ever wondered what God thinks of those people who deny his existence or the fact that he is God of the universe? Of those who propagate untruths through books and the media and in their teaching? He loves them. Have you ever considered what God thinks of immoral people? He loves them. What might God think of those who oppress others? He loves them. He loves them all, the oppressed and the oppressors. What does God think of thieves and cheats and liars and drunks? He loves them. Of people in business? He loves them. Of parents at home? He loves them. How does God respond to an indifferent world? He loves it! That's the size of agape love. Agape can love an indifferent world.

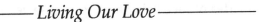

————————— *Living Our Love* —————————

List the five most unlovable people you know. Pray specifically for each of them, so that God's love can be released to work in their lives.

# God loves the world, but he doesn't like it!

> For God so loved the world that he gave his one
> and only Son, that whoever believes in him shall
> not perish but have eternal life.    —*John 3:16*

Imagine this rendition of the above verse: "God so loved the world that he was sentimental about it," or "God so loved the world that he had a romantic feeling about it," or "God so loved the world that he had a friendly tolerance without conviction, and it didn't really matter what the world did," or "God so liked the world . . ."

When the Bible says that "God is love," it isn't necessarily saying that God likes us an awful lot. We've got to throw out our old idea of love being a more intense version of like. We must keep the concept in mind that God's love and the Christian's love is primarily concerned with the well-being of the beloved. If we define love as "liking someone a lot," look what happens to the truths of Scripture. If, instead of loving, God just liked the world a lot, wouldn't he just decide to make more worlds? If you ate a pizza you liked a lot, you might order another one. If you have a favorite purple scarf, you might go out and purchase a similar red one. Why not?

John 3:16 doesn't say, "God liked the world so much, he created several more just like it." Instead it says, basically, "God so loved the world that he disliked intensely." God disliked the attitude of the world; he disliked what the world's population had done to his earth; he disliked intensely the rebuff he had received from the world; and he disliked intensely what was happening to his world as a result of that rebuff. What really happened was that God looked at the world—this world of sin and sinners—and disliked in-

14

tensely what he saw. But he made a decision to love—to be primarily concerned for the well-being of what he didn't like. He disliked it all intensely, and loved it all to distraction!

So the love of God goes beyond liking—in fact has nothing to do with liking. The love of God is a total commitment to something he doesn't like at all. It's really a mind-boggling concept: to love is to make a decision to be primarily concerned with the well-being of that which you may not even like. This is the way God loves the world.

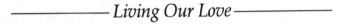

————— *Living Our Love* —————

Read and meditate on Isaiah 1.

# Agape—God's steadfast love

> I will betroth you to me forever; I will betroth you
> in righteousness and justice, in love and
> compassion. I will betroth you in faithfulness, and
> you will acknowledge the LORD. . . . I will show my
> love to the one I called "Not my loved one." I will
> say to those called "Not my people" "You are my
> people"; and they will say, "You are my God."
>
> —*Hosea 2:19-20, 23*

Thomas Aquinas said, "Creation sprang from God's love of giving." The people God created knew that God cared. And if God cared, he loved. Enoch walked with God, knowing the personal love of God. So did Noah. So did Abraham, through whom God's redemptive love for humankind was revealed and from whom a nation called Israel came into being. One hundred and seventy-one times in the Old Testament we read about God's "steadfast love"—*hesed*—for his people. Psalm 136 talks about his steadfast love enduring forever.

This passage in Hosea describes love that would take back a wife who had been unfaithful. In fact, the prophet Hosea had just such a wife; he ended up buying her back and bringing her home to be his wife again. God used this painful situation to illustrate the nature of his kind of love for us—*hesed*.

In the New Testament the equivalent word is *agape*. Agape love is altruistic love. The good news is that "God is agape." If God were *eros* (erotic love), he would possess us and consume us—and grow cold if we were to ever be unfaithful. If God were *philia* (sentimental love), he would have given up on us the minute we gave up on him. Because God is agape, he has committed himself totally and eternally to being concerned with our well-being, irrespective of our condition and regardless of our reaction.

Agape is a sober, thought-out position. Agape expresses a deep and constant love, the interest of a perfect being toward entirely unworthy objects. And agape takes action instead of wishing things would turn out all right.

So agape love stems from the very character of God. It's a matter of principle, duty, rightness. It is one of his attributes. God doesn't *have* love; he *is* love, and his love is directed unrelentingly toward us—undeserving as we are.

We're talking about God's kind of love—not love as the world thinks of it—the gooey, flavorless, Hollywood variety of the I-love-you-today and I-don't-love-you-tomorrow. Nothing like that.

Agape is out of this world!

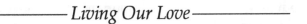 *Living Our Love*

Describe a time when you have been made surprisingly aware of God's agape love.

# Love isn't a feeling

> A new command I give you: Love one another. As I
> have loved you, so you must love one another.
>
> —*John 13:34*

The above verse is quoted quite frequently. But have you
ever considered what these words imply? We are commanded
to love.

How can God command a feeling? He can't. The love God
asks for is not primarily a feeling; it is a decision.

When we set out to try to love God with our whole heart,
it's easy to feel guilty because we don't "feel" like we love
God. We can't work ourselves up emotionally to love him. But
the whole point is that feelings aren't essential. Feelings enter
in, but they are not the most important part. To love God is to
obey him, to seek his will.

So it is in the realm of decisions, the deepest part, where
our Christian life has to be lived. It's just like marriage. If you
live your marriage in the realm of emotions alone, it will be a
rocky ride. It will be an up-and-down experience along with
your feelings. Marriage is meant to be lived on the solid base
of our decisions. We commit ourselves—that's agape love.
Feelings come and go, commitments stand firm. If we live our
marriages in the realm of emotions alone we are choosing
the shallowest part of us. We all pass through times when
our feelings are stormy, but if the commitment is strong, we
will have a marriage built in the realm of decision—the
deepest part.

Feelings will run out of a marriage, sooner or later. There
will always come a time when sexual attraction will decline,
and family affection cannot carry the strain. Feelings won't go
the distance. All the more reason for us to obey the impulses

of agape. This is the way to tasting the greatest love and togetherness in marriage.

Remember Paul's command to married people not to withhold sexual relationship from one another? There are times when our feelings would dictate isolation instead of togetherness—and a loving partner respects the way his or her spouse feels. But intimacy is meant to be maintained. And this is where agape steps in, as both parties review and renew their commitments to meet each other's needs. Then the feelings will return. There are other times when family affection is practically nonexistent. If we were to admit it, there are times when we really don't *like* our children very much—or our spouse. We're annoyed at their habits, tired of their demands. But agape keeps us going. Agape is not primarily feelings; it's commitment, it's decision, it's obedience. If we could only learn this, how many families would be preserved, rather than torn apart? How many relationships could grow strong over the years, rather than disintegrate?

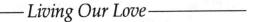

——————— *Living Our Love* ———————

Make a list of family members you don't "feel" you love. Think and pray about making a commitment to be "primarily concerned with their well-being"—no matter what the cost to yourself.

# Love, lust, and laughter

> But among you there must not be even a hint of
> sexual immorality, or of any kind of impurity, or of
> greed, because these are improper for God's holy
> people. Nor should there be obscenity, foolish talk
> or coarse joking, which are out of place, but rather
> thanksgiving. . . . For you were once darkness, but
> now you are light in the Lord. . . . Have nothing to
> do with the fruitless deeds of darkness, but rather
> expose them. For it is shameful even to mention
> what the disobedient do in secret.
>
> —*Ephesians 5:3-4, 8, 11-12*

The most beautiful thing in all the universe is love. In our
society it is in danger of becoming the most perverted and
sordid thing imaginable. The rank perversion of love should
give us great concern.

Often in the very area where love is supposed to be demonstrated, there is heartache and friction and envy and jealousy and strife. There is selfishness instead of sacrifice. There
is hardness instead of forgiveness. An obdurate attitude has
replaced the overflow of love. We are guilty of perverting that
which God wants to perfect in our lives.

The Christians in Ephesus were living in a climate of perversion. It showed up in perverted conduct and perverted
conversation. It was particularly evident in this case with
conduct that misunderstood sex and in conversation that
abused sex.

Sex is beautiful when legitimate. Love is expressed and
sublimated in the sex act. But love without legality is not true
love; it smacks more of lust. The sheer perversion of this
glorious thing that God has shed abroad in our world, love,

is seen in contemporary attitudes toward sex without marriage. We are engaging in sex outside of the legitimate areas in which God has designed it to function. This is symptomatic of the depths to which we are falling, the immensity of the perversion.

Paul gets specific about this topic. He talks about fornication, uncleanness, and covetousness. He teaches that it shouldn't even be discussed among the believers! Not in the sense of talking responsibly about it—as he was doing. But he means that Christians should not be entertaining thoughts of sexual immorality or impurity in their minds. Paul found it necessary to teach bluntly about this in his day, and we live in similar days and need to take similar stances. Even in the church of Christ immorality and impurity and rank indulgence are seen on every hand. Even believers appear to be confusing love and lust.

What God condemns as lust, fornication, uncleanness, and covetousness—in other words, sex that is outside of monogamous, heterosexual marriage, basically seeking its own satisfaction—has nothing to do with the love of God that should be rampant in Christians' lives.

Paul also discusses perversion of love in conversation. This is important, because in many instances, there is a lot of talking going on—more talking than acting, particularly when you get into locker room talk. There is a wonderful opportunity here for the Christian to show that he is not even remotely interested in love's perversion. Paul says: "Nor should there be obscenity, foolish talk or coarse joking, which are out of place, but thanksgiving."

When Paul mentions "foolish talk," he uses a word we could translate "moronic." There is no question that a lot of sex talk that goes on around us as we move in our society is completely moronic. Don't have anything to do with this kind of talk because it is an utter perversion of the most glorious thing that God has given: love itself.

Next Paul talks about "joking." You may be thinking, *Oh no! That means that I can't tell any more jokes or have a good laugh ever again.* That's not what Paul is talking about. The word really means "turning something around." We might call it the "double entendre" or "double meaning." You've gotten yourself into situations where you've said something perfectly innocently and it's been twisted by someone else's dirty thinking. You can't avoid that happening, but you can, and should, have nothing to do with promoting or employing it.

This is yet another perversion of God's beautiful gift of love. We live in a society that is filthy in its thinking and foolish in its talking. And the apostle Paul encourages us to understand love's perfection and have nothing to do with love's perversion.

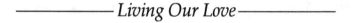

## ——————— *Living Our Love* ———————

Ask the Holy Spirit to show you where love has become perverted in your life.

# Eros abused

Let him kiss me with the kisses of his mouth—
for your love is more delightful than wine.
Pleasing is the fragrance of your perfumes;
your name is like perfume poured out.
No wonder the maidens love you!
Take me away with you—let us hurry!
Let the king bring me into his chambers.
—*Song of Solomon 1:2-4*

*Eros* is one of the Greek words for love. It concerns our sexuality. It is the erotic aspect of love. Christians have seen the abuse of eros—the abuse of erotic things. And many Christians have raised a protest about the abuses of eros. But, seeing the abuse, they sometimes overlook the fact that is fundamental—that erotic love is something that God invented and ordained and gave to us as a gift. But God recognized the sheer power of eros-love, and so he determined that restrictions had to be placed on it. What Christians should rightly stand against is the absence of those restraints.

The Bible is clear: Erotic love belongs within the confines of marriage. Christians can stand against the abuses of eros while affirming the true validity of erotic, sexual love within the boundaries God ordained. It's as straightforward as that. Think of it this way: every red-blooded male has the erotic and physiological capability to populate a small town! That's alarming! So God instituted a fundamental control: We must exercise our erotic, sexual love capability exclusively within the confines of marriage.

Christians tend to sweep the topic of erotic love under the carpet because they are uncomfortable with it. We need to keep in mind that the "bad" aspect of eros is not the fact that it relates to sex, but that it doesn't relate much to anything but self. Eros is basically egotistical; it longs to possess something it desires and to derive satisfaction from possessing that which it desires. This is valid within marriage, but it's dangerous when it is not balanced by the other aspects of love that should characterize the marriage covenant. And when the Bible teaches us about loving one another, and that "God is love," it isn't referring to eros.

Eros is beautiful when agape love rules over it and draws up the conditions. But without help, eros can become a demon—guilty of murder and rape and other societal ills.

Though sex alone isn't love, the idea that sex is love is commonly held. And it's not just something adults develop—it's a point of view propagated among our youth. When our kids were young, I asked them to "collect" sayings off the t-shirts worn by teenagers. I was interested in what kids in the upper grades of elementary school through high school were wearing on their shirts. Some blatantly displayed the most coarse four-letter words. One worn by a junior high student proclaimed, "I'm a virgin—but this is a very old t-shirt." Many high schoolers wore ones that read, "Let your fingers do the walking!" The attitudes conveyed by these messages leads to sex without love and the serious problems of sexually transmitted diseases, teen pregnancy, single parenting, and abortion.

Look at so many relationships today. People tend to expect that mere feeling will do all that is necessary. That's eros. Eros might say, "Oh, I mean it! I will love you always!" Always is eternal, and human love isn't eternal. A young girl wrote to me, "I didn't want to go to bed with him, but he pushed me. But when I gave in, he lost interest. For him, it was the end. For me, it was the beginning. I can't understand it." What a tragedy! Eros had blazed and died for him because it was not controlled by agape love. He went on his merry way, satisfied; she stayed and sobbed, violated and forlorn. Real love sets boundaries. Eros love has to be protected for our own good.

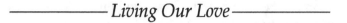

## *Living Our Love*

Watch a married couple who has been together in a strong, spiritual marriage for some time. How does their behavior toward each other demonstrate more than an eros kind of love? How can we help young people to understand eros and to behave appropriately?

# A story of love gone wrong

> King Solomon, however, loved many foreign
> women besides Pharaoh's daughter—Moabites,
> Ammonites, Edomites, Sidonians and Hittites. They
> were from nations about which the LORD had told
> the Israelites, "You must not intermarry with them,
> because they will surely turn your hearts after their
> gods." Nevertheless, Solomon held fast to them in
> love. He had seven hundred wives of royal birth
> and three hundred concubines, and his wives led
> him astray. As Solomon grew old, his wives turned
> his heart after other gods, and his heart was not
> fully devoted to the LORD his God, as the heart of
> David his father had been.       —1 Kings 11:1-4

We know a pretty young woman with two beautiful children. She and her husband were missionaries for a number of years. They did a marvelous work for God. Then they joined a social club, and there he fell in love with another woman—after fourteen years on the mission field. For the last two years he has come home for breakfast, gone to work, returned for dinner, and then spent the night with this other woman. It really is hell for his wife. This man told us, "But it's for love's sake! I'm doing it for love's sake." Love is god in that believer's life, and it has become a demon in that family. As C.S. Lewis says, love becomes a demon the moment it becomes a god.

You see, eros (the "in-love" part) needs divine help. Without God it either dies or becomes a demon. Erotic love needs divine control, divine boundaries. Obedience to agape love will command us to do certain things about our human loves. For example, I have no doubt that the young missionary "loves" both women, because eros, the in-love love, happens to all of us. It even happens to married people. It is quite possible—and not an uncommon occurrence—to be "in love" with more than one person at a time. We don't doubt that this man is "in love." But what should he do about it? If he loves God first, then he should obey the rules of agape love and say no to his human love, no matter how he feels.

We see this same sad story happen again and again—and among Christians, who should understand better than the world what agape love is all about. We are always in need of God's grace, and agape love is definitely a part of God's grace. But it cannot help us if we ignore its requirements: to put ahead of everything else the well-being of the person to whom we are committed.

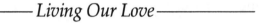

## —————— Living Our Love ——————

What should you do if you feel sexually attracted to someone who is not your spouse? How does an understanding of eros and agape help?

# Boy meets girl

> How good and pleasant it is when brothers live
> together in unity! . . . It is as if the dew of Hermon
> were falling on Mount Zion. For there the LORD
> bestows his blessing, even life forevermore.
>
> —*Psalm 133:1, 3*

The Greek love word, *philia*, carries the idea of friendship or relationship, the idea of acquaintanceship or brotherhood. It includes the romantic and sentimental. It is not egotistic love—like eros, which basically seeks satisfaction for inner drives. It is a mutualistic love, love that responds to love. Anyone familiar with Hollywood has seen the following scenario.

> Boy meets girl.
> Boy: "I like you."
> Girl: "I like *you*."
> Boy: "I like you more than I said."
> Girl: "I like *you* more than I said."
> Boy: "I like you a *lot*."
> Girl: "I like *you* a lot."
> Boy: "I *love* you."
> Girl: "What!?"
> Boy: "Nothing."
> Girl: "Go on."
> Boy: "I love you."
> Girl: "I love *you*."
> Boy: "You do?"
> Girl: "I do."

The relationship is mutualistic and escalating. The outcome is obvious. These two will marry and live happily ever after—for at least five or six weeks!

Philia is a different kind of love than eros because it goes beyond the egotistic to be mutualistic. Basically it says: "I like you because you like me because I like you." It builds and feeds upon itself—on its own momentum.

But mutualistic love reaches a limit and may de-escalate in the same way that it escalates. Mutualistic love can't stick it out in the long run. One of the saddest truths of today's society, both within and without Christianity, is that we have numerous marriages that have never gone beyond a stage of mutualistic love. And those couples can't survive. Why? Because philia is a needy kind of love. It needs to be needed. It gives because it wants to receive.

Philia love can also de-escalate in nonromantic friendships and within our families. As children grow up and become their own persons, some parents discover how little real agape love they have for their offspring! How many families do you know in which relationships have broken down altogether, despite family ties? How many friendships have become broken because one or the other person decided he or she wasn't "getting enough out of it"? Mutual loving is good, but it still falls short of agape love—the love that says I love you whether you're beautiful or pretty, whether you do what I want. Philia loves in return; agape loves even when there is no return.

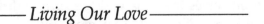

## Living Our Love

Think of the love you've shared with friends and family. What have been the shortcomings of that kind of love? Where has it disappointed you?

# Do we·really love him?

> The third time [Jesus] said to him, "Simon son of
> John, do you truly love me?" Peter was hurt
> because Jesus asked him the third time, "Do you
> love me?" He said, "Lord, you know all things; you
> know that I love you."                    —*John 21:17*

After his resurrection, Jesus asks Peter, "Do you love me?"
He is asking, "Do you *agape* me? Do you love me as I love
you?" Peter had recently discovered that he didn't, though he
had thought before that he did. He answers truthfully, "No, I
*philia* you. I am fond of you. I have tender affection for you. I
have a human love for you." Peter, sitting beside a charcoal
fire, was probably remembering the last time he'd sat near
such a fire, when he'd denied knowing the Lord Jesus. He
remembered vividly that he did not *agape* Jesus Christ then.
But Jesus kept asking, "Do you *agape* me? Do you *agape* me?
This is what I desire from you. This is what the law and the
prophets were all about. This is what God came to earth to
tell us, that he wants us to *agape* him." To *philia* God was not
enough.

Human love is bound to come short of the mark when the
heat is on. Peter panicked. The late hour, the arrest in Gethsemane, the threatening circumstances that were developing for
Jesus and his friends—all contributed to the denial. Many of
us find ourselves by a charcoal fire surrounded by family,
classmates, or colleagues. That pressures us to reveal our
allegiance to Christ. If we act in agape love we will be more
concerned with Christ's good name than ours! We will not
deny we know him.

But if we fail or act in philia love he will forgive us. If we
are willing he will meet us at the place of failure, just as he

met Peter, and he will give us a chance to be honest and confess our shortcomings. Then he will give us something to do for him. Failure, after all, is never final for a Christian.

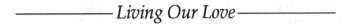

## *Living Our Love*

Has there been a time in your life when you felt that you have denied the Lord? Come to Christ in prayer— you will find him eager and ready to forgive.

# Doing what comes naturally

> Those who live according to the sinful nature have
> their minds set on what that nature desires; but
> those who live in accordance with the Spirit have
> their minds set on what the Spirit desires. The mind
> of sinful man is death, but the mind controlled by
> the Spirit is life and peace; the sinful mind is hostile
> to God. It does not submit to God's law, nor can it
> do so. Those controlled by the sinful nature cannot
> please God.
> —*Romans 8:5-8*

I (Jill) remember as a child arguing with my sister Shirley a lot. Somebody asked my mother once, "Do they blend, Peggy, do they blend?" Well, we didn't blend. Maybe you have a sister like that. I remember once when we were very small my father giving Shirley two sixpences, one for each of us. And I remember Shirley telling me she had lost mine! As a four- or five-year-old I tried to figure out what was so unfair about that. How did she know it was *my* sixpence? I wondered. I mean, weren't they absolutely identical? But that's what happens when you are children. Selfishness is one of the first things parents have to train *out* of their children, for it comes quite naturally.

Usually when children are arguing and come crying to a parent saying that something is "not fair," they don't really mean that it's not fair. They mean that the situation is no longer to their advantage. They're selfish, and they want you to take their side. They don't want you to be fair and impartial. Quite simply, it's against their nature.

That's natural, you say. It's sort of cute. Well, God doesn't think it's sort of cute, but God does see it as our natural bent. Human beings see the "natural" as basically good. Yet only

God is good. And if someone is natural, God says that's the person's main problem. They need the new birth. They need to become spiritual.

There's an epitaph on a gravestone in England. It says:

Here lies a miser who lived for himself,
lived for nothing but gathering wealth.
Now where he is and how he fares,
nobody knows and nobody cares.

What a terrible thing. If that man was truly so self-centered, there's a dreadful possibility he's living now in total isolation, for I believe that's what hell is: living with yourself for all eternity. Nobody else will be there, just your thoroughly selfish self, separated from God, apart from any good company at all. In fact, it isn't really true that "where he is and how he fares, nobody knows and nobody cares," for the Bible teaches and Jesus said that we'll all be separated from him forever if we do not let Jesus do something about our natural state.

The world may say that "natural" is good, but Christians cannot believe that if they have any knowledge at all of sin—and its selfish consequences.

 *Living Our Love*

As you go through the next two days, try to be conscious of your *natural* responses to being treated rudely, not doing well at some task, having unexpected company, and so forth. How do you think God's love would differ from your responses?

# The power of love

You see, just at the right time, when we were still powerless, Christ died for the ungodly. —*Romans 5:6*

I have the desire to do what is good, but I cannot carry it out. For what I do is not the good I want to do; the evil I do not want to do—this I keep on doing. —*Romans 7:18-19*

$P$aul understood the meaning of powerlessness. We are powerless to change our condition, powerless to reconcile ourselves to God. We are powerless to live lives that are up to the level of God's glory, powerless to equip ourselves for eternity, powerless to make ourselves fit for heaven. We are powerless to stop doing the things that deep down we would like to stop doing, and powerless to do the things that we commit ourselves to doing. We are powerless to undo what we've done, to do retroactively what we should have done. We're in a mess—and powerless!

*Powerless* is not a very popular word during this century of woman power, black power, gay power, etc. Power is what everybody wants—even if they have to get it by force! And, unfortunately, we often confuse forcefulness with power. But the Bible is clear that, whatever power is, we don't possess enough of it to change our own lives.

We have considerable intellectual ability and considerable technological know-how. There's no question that human beings are remarkable creatures and have achieved great things. But the problem is that although we can send a man to the moon and bring him back again, we are powerless to make him fit to live on earth. Look at humankind's history. People have tried to make life a better experience, they have tried to love and be strong, but ultimately they have encountered defeat. We have great psychological power, even great creative power and physical power, but—because of sin—we do not have moral, spiritual power. Consequently, we are powerless when it comes to living and expressing true, agape love.

But Paul makes the point in the next few verses of Romans 5 that *while we were in that condition* Christ died for us because God loves us. That's the wonderful good news of the gospel. This is why Jesus had to come, to live, die, and rise again—so that we could have access to *God's* power. In Jesus Christ we do have power—and the power to love.

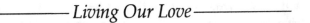

## Living Our Love

Think about an area of your life that needs changing by spiritual power. Thank God that the power to change is accessible by the Holy Spirit.

# Loving by the Holy Spirit

> I will ask the Father, and he will give you another
> Counselor to be with you forever—the Spirit of
> truth.
> —*John 14:16-17*

You cannot truly love God or people in a way that pleases God without the Holy Spirit.

The Holy Spirit is a person. This is what Jesus said about the Holy Spirit: "[The Father] will give you another Counselor to be with you forever—the Spirit of truth" (John 14:16-17). The idea is of One exactly like himself, who is called alongside to help. Jesus was going away, but he was going to give the Spirit of truth to stay with the believer forever. "I will not leave you as orphans; I will come to you" (14:18). Jesus promises, "If anyone loves me, he will obey my teaching. My Father will love him, and we will come to him and make our home with him" (14:23).

When the Holy Spirit comes, he will pour out the agape love of God into our hearts (Romans 5:5). He provides the love we need to control our human loves and to love God fully. We can't do it without the Holy Spirit. That's one of the points of 1 Corinthians 13:1-3. You can *do* all sorts of things—become a martyr, give up all you have, do good works. But without the Holy Spirit of love you can't love God the way he requires it.

The Holy Spirit won't sneak into your life when you're not watching. He doesn't seep into your body and heart. He's a person, and he must be invited. The promise of the love of God poured into our hearts in Romans 5:5 is preceded by verses that explain that first we must be justified by faith and receive him willingly.

If the Holy Spirit is resident in our hearts, then why do we have churches full of people who profess to know God but lack love? Here's a handy little saying to explain it: Because the Holy Spirit is resident, but he isn't president! Not only do we not allow him to be in control, we often resist him, quench him, grieve him, and insult him. The Holy Spirit can come into a believer's life and still be grieved and quenched, resisted and insulted.

The Holy Spirit does not come into our hearts to do his deepest work in the shallowest part of us, which is our emotions. He will touch our emotions, but emotions come and go. He wants to do his deepest work in our deepest part—in our spiritual decisions, in our discipling, in our wills. If we have decided to love God with all our hearts—that's the Holy Spirit's work! When we even say, "I want to love God," the Holy Spirit has worked to make us want to. We are so helpless, so powerless without his help.

And so if you want to be a loving person, you cannot be the truly loving person you should be and God created you to be without the Holy Spirit. For the love of God is shed abroad, or scattered around, in our hearts by the Holy Spirit. There is no other way. You can't work it up or manufacture it.

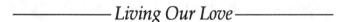

## Living Our Love

When have you tried to love but have forgotten to rely on the Holy Spirit loving through you?

# Two approaches to love

"The fruit of the Spirit is love. . . . "     —*Galatians 5:22*

A new commandment I give you: Love one another.
                                            —*John 13:34*

Spiritual truths tend to impress us when they coordinate with our differing personalities. Some people say, "Love is a fruit of the Holy Spirit. If you love, it'll be as a result of the Holy Spirit loving people through you that you can't love." And that can be helpful to people with a somewhat passive nature. Passive people will simply sit back and trust the *Holy Spirit* to produce love through them that they can't produce.

Yet another person would say, "What? Do you mean to say that you'd just stand there, being all passive, and expect that the Holy Spirit is supposed to do all the work? Then why on earth didn't God just give the Holy Spirit the Bible and not bother giving it to us!?" Active-approach people focus on love as a commandment not to the Holy Spirit but to *believers*. Active-approach people feel that if they're not loving others it's simply a matter of getting down to just obeying God and doing it.

These two types of Christians can disagree on—even fight over—the very topic of love! Whichever side you personally have taken, understand that you may be wrong—because you are only partly right. As we Christians do not have the luxury of choosing which side of this fence to be on because God teaches *both*. We can't approach Scripture selectively on the basis of obeying what appeals to us and bypassing what seems too difficult to tackle. God doesn't give us that choice.

If you're primarily passive in outlook, you might get carried away by pursuing some emotional experience of the

Holy Spirit that will flood you with love. And until you have that experience you feel that it's perfectly all right to remain awkward and irritable and disinterested in people because you are waiting for that spiritual experience.

If you're primarily active in approach, you might be so active you drive yourself nuts trying to love—trying to love the unlovely, trying to love the unlovable, trying to love unloving people. You get more and more frustrated with them and—deep down—with yourself.

The answer is to marry these two approaches by concentrating on the one that doesn't come naturally. If I'm passive naturally and automatically drawn to the teaching of the blessed Holy Spirit in mighty power filling my heart with love, then I don't need to concentrate on the Holy Spirit. I need to concentrate on being obedient—approaching people in the power of the Holy Spirit and cultivating a loving attitude.

On the other hand, if I'm an active sort of person who knows what it's like to be obedient but I'm frustrated because my obedience isn't getting me anywhere, what I've got to do is concentrate on the blessed ministry of the Holy Spirit. I need to pray, "O Holy Spirit, I've sought to be obedient, but I'm not seeing results. I'm frustrating myself and those around me. I need to know what it is to depend on you to enable me to be what I'm not and do what I can't."

The sheer practicality of marrying the two approaaches is that if I'm ever going to establish love as a goal and pursue it relentlessly, it will take obedience to God's command and dependence on God's Spirit. There is no shortcut.

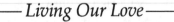 *Living Our Love*

Which approach of loving comes most naturally to you?
How can you put the other approach into practice?

# Love is the primary goal

Follow the way of love.                    —*1 Corinthians 14:1*

Perhaps the best-known expression Paul uses concerning goal setting in the life of a believer is found in 1 Corinthians 14:1—a simple expression, but full of profound meaning.

The phrase "follow the way" can also mean "to pursue, press toward, hunt down." What he's saying is that Christians should establish goals in their lives, but the paramount goal is the one of adopting a loving lifestyle and being committed to a loving approach to people. We could paraphrase Paul's teaching as, "Establish love as a goal, and pursue it relentlessly."

We often miss the fact that these words form the conclusion to the whole preceding chapter—the famous "love chapter." First Corinthians 13 actually climaxes in chapter 14, verse 1. The person who separated Paul's teaching into chapters separated important teaching from its important climax, and readers unfortunately can comfortably study the whole of chapter 13 and sit back and say, "Oh, isn't that nice" and never notice that the whole point of the exposition of love is found in the important command to "follow the way of love!"

Put 1 Corinthians 14:1 where it belongs, and you see that Paul is saying, "As the result of all that I'm teaching you here about love in chapter 13, now establish love as a goal and pursue it relentlessly." All that he has taught about love is basically that it is absolutely paramount—that any believer building a realistically Christian lifestyle *must* build the characteristic of love into it. I must recognize the necessity of establishing realistic, biblical goals. Then I must give myself to the fact that goals are important, and the paramount one is the goal of love. But we must bear in mind that this goal is totally unattainable without the Spirit.

—————— *Living Our Love* ——————

What kinds of "goals" can you set for love this week?

# Love demonstrated in Christ

> Now Christ is the visible expression of the invisible
> God. . . . It was in him that the full nature of God
> chose to live, and through him God planned to
> reconcile to his own person everything on earth and
> everything in Heaven, making peace by virtue of
> Christ's death on the cross.
>
> —*Colossians 1:15, 19-20* (PHILLIPS)

> Your attitude should be the same as that of
>   Christ Jesus:
> Who, being in very nature God,
> did not consider equality with God something
>   to be grasped,
> but made himself nothing,
> taking the very nature of a servant,
> being made in human likeness.          —*Philippians 2:5-7*

Isn't it fantastic that God could show us himself through
another human being? It sounds impossible, yet that is exactly
what God did. We can know what God is like by looking at
the life of Jesus. So, if we want to know about agape love
shown in human lives, we should spend some time learning
from Jesus Christ.

Paul painted a stunning picture of Jesus' agape love in
Philippians, chapter 2. Not only does this passage describe
Jesus' character, but it tells the amazing story of God come
to earth.

In heaven, you see, Jesus was fully recognized as coequal
with God. Honor was his by eternal right. Yet he didn't
consider that something to be "grasped" or held on to. Insist-
ing on his rights was not his approach. He had every reason

to be proud, every reason to stay in heaven. He was omnipotent, omniscient. He was free from all restraints, self-existent, utterly sufficient, transcending all spatial limits (omnipresent). He had a good thing going there in heaven: security, good prospects, no rain, no snow, no fear, no pain, no sorrow, no death. He was part of a Trinity of loving unity. The angels adored him; cherubim and seraphim veiled their faces before him. Christ was the light of heaven, as well as the light of the world.

And he let it all go for people who were opposed to all that he stood for. We call that love!

> And being found in appearance as a man,
> he humbled himself
> and became obedient to death—
> even death on a cross!
> —*Philippians 2:8*

That's agape love. He laid aside the outer trappings of his glorious deity and clothed himself with humanity. Throughout his life, Jesus turned from the dignity of deity and lived in the midst of the depravity of humanity. He dealt with us on our own ignorant, faithless, fearful level. He could have had anything in all of heaven or earth. Instead, he chose us. To live among us, die for us. That's love!

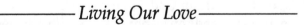

## *Living Our Love*

What have you given up in your life for the sake of loving others? What kinds of sacrifices have you seen others make?

# Love needs hands and feet

> Therefore, I urge you, brothers, in view of God's
> mercy, to offer your bodies as living sacrifices, holy
> and pleasing to God—this is your spiritual act of
> worship. Do not conform any longer to the pattern
> of this world, but be transformed by the renewing
> of your mind. Then you will be able to test and
> approve what God's will is—his good, pleasing and
> perfect will.                                        —*Romans 12:1-2*

Lord, I want my body to be well cared for. I don't want to present you with a flabby mass that can't get up in the morning to worship you, travel distances to preach for you, or work hard to keep my house decent, my kids fed, clothed, and happy, and still have enough energy left to go to a ballgame with the family. I want to present to you a body that's healthy and vigorous, as you enable me, because loving is done through bodies. It needs hands and feet.

I want people to look at me and say, "Is that a Christian?" If we're so spiritual that we ignore the physical, what good is that going to do? When Paul says "offer your bodies to God," he had active service in mind. So let's get into shape.

We need to give to God a healthy sacrifice, a holy sacrifice: "Present your bodies a living sacrifice, wholly acceptable unto God." Set apart for God. Loving is sacrificial. It takes its toll. It makes demands on us physically, spiritually, and emotionally. Some people say this being set apart and presenting ourselves sacrificially is something additional in the Christian life—for those who are so inclined. They say that you need to get converted, keep church and God in a little compartment, and the rest of your life is your own.

But the Bible says we're to be set apart for God. We need to be people healthy enough and whole enough and holy enough for him to use. After all, he has so much loving for us to do out in this hurting world, and we need some health and energy in order to do it.

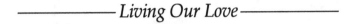
*Living Our Love*

What are the distinctive qualities of health, wholeness, and holiness?

# Doing what comes spiritually

> The Word of the LORD came to Jonah, son of Amittai:
> "Go to the great city of Nineveh and preach against
> it, because its wickedness has come up before me."
> But Jonah ran away from the Lord.  —*Jonah 1:1-3*

When Stuart and I first came to Elmbrook Church, I struggled over being involved with women's ministries. Teenagers had always been my forte. I loved kids, and I knew from past experience that I could work with them effectively. But God began to give me opportunities to teach women.

I took some of those opportunities, but I had an attitude problem like Jonah's—well, maybe not *quite* so angry. And the more I ministered to women, the more I was asked to do. My attitude resulted in me feeling even more distant from the women. Like Jonah, I gritted my teeth and said, "All right, I'll do it because I've got to. I'll do it to obey God." But there was no love there, and the women I spoke to must have been aware of it.

Then one day, a dear friend sat me down and said, "Jill, you have God-given abilities, but you don't love these women." Faithful are the wounds of a friend! She was right, but I was stubborn. Finally, I prayed in repentance that God would give me his agape love. I prayed that, whether or not he ever gave me chances to speak again, the women might know that I loved them.

And I do. That's the miracle. That's what happens when the love of God is shed abroad in your heart by the Holy Spirit. He is in control. He gives the special ability to love beyond yourself. Without the control of his love, gifts are empty and ineffective.

How many Christians do you think just "naturally" want to work with the homeless, with AIDS patients, with behavior-disordered children, with people on drugs? The only way God can minister to all the needs in the world is for us to say, "I'm willing, Lord, to love whomever needs it. But it has to be your love; without it, this situation only frustrates, discourages, and disgusts me."

In fact, often the people who are really gifted in a certain area—such as youth work or music or whatever—actually go along for some time under their own steam, never relying on God's agape love to fill them, and never reaching their potential. Real love for people is a gift directly from the heart of God: a gift that is released as we trust him and obey. We must never forget that.

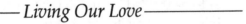

## *Living Our Love*

If you can pray this simple prayer, God can do great things through you: "Lord, I am willing to be shaped by your love, and to love whom you lead me to serve in love."

# Love fellowships with God

> Blessed is the man who does not walk in the
> counsel of the wicked or stand in the way of sinners
> or sit in the seat of mockers. But his delight is in the
> law of the LORD, and on his law he meditates day
> and night.                                    —*Psalm 1:1-2*

The person who loves is one who has a desire for God. This psalm goes on to say that this person "is like a tree planted by streams of water, which yields its fruit in its season and whose leaf does not wither." What a beautiful picture. To this person, being in the presence of God is a delight, not a duty.

Is it a duty to read the Bible? Is it a duty to love Jesus? Is it a duty just to be thrilled about God your Father? Love seeks fellowship with God by its very nature.

But often, even in our great desire to relate deeply to God, we feel frustrated. Sometimes we get glimpses of what God is truly like, but it's very difficult to get a clear picture, and it's hard to love someone whom you only have a fuzzy picture of.

But in eternity, love, by its very nature, will be in *full* communication with God. As Paul says in 1 Corinthians 13:12, "Now we see but a poor reflection as in a mirror; then we shall see face to face. Now I know in part; then I shall know fully, even as I am fully known."

Paul uses this word *mirror*, but in his day people didn't have glass mirrors. They only had pieces of highly polished bronze or copper. And when they looked in it they saw only an imperfect reflection.

The idea of the "poor reflection" could be more accurately translated with the English words *enigma* or *riddle* or *puzzle*. You can imagine Paul carrying a small pocket piece of bronze.

When he looked into it he saw a poor reflection of himself. An enigma. Poor Paul never really knew what he looked like!

That's how it is here on earth. This side of glory we don't understand—even as we exercise our gifts and see the way God is using us. If we try our hardest to fathom out all that God is and all that God is doing, the best we can do is no better than the puzzle of a reflection in a poorly polished bit of bronze.

The good news is that one day we will see God face to face. One day we can throw out the polished piece of bronze and fully comprehend and experience total communication. Love is what urges us to look forward to that great knowing. And love is what will make that knowing possible. We could never enjoy fellowship with God if he had not first decided—because of his great love—to have fellowship with us.

## Living Our Love

What kinds of things do you do with a person you just enjoy being around? What activities can you do that help you to fellowship with God?

# Gifts are limited—but love is not

> Love never fails. But where there are prophecies,
> they will cease; where there are tongues, they will
> be stilled; where there is knowledge, it will pass
> away. For we know in part and we prophecy in
> part, but when perfection comes, the imperfect
> disappears. —1 Corinthians 13:8-10

The apostle Paul says here that love is far more important than gifts because gifts are so limited. It's only a matter of time until spiritual gifts become obsolete. When they have served their purposes they will cease. But love will still be relevant. Gifts will be abolished, love will always be needed. Glory will mean total completion—and love will mean total comprehension.

We know only in a limited way; we speak in a limited way; we exercise our gifts in a limited way, but there is unlimited truth in God. For this reason, don't value spiritual gifts more highly than love. They must be seen within the divine, eternal perspective. So, too, must love.

Spiritual gifts are also limited by those who have received them. God gives wonderful gifts to people who are, frankly, not so wonderful. A bad attitude can decrease a gift's potential. A sinful lifestyle can call its exercise into question. It only takes a little virus for the gifted person to be laid flat on his back, and the gift lies dormant. It is still a great gift, but one little problem in the person who has been gifted can make it useless.

For example, a gifted preacher may develop nodules on his vocal chords, rendering his gifts inoperative. Gifts are so easily flattened. The gift is invested in a limited human being, and that human being could suffer any setback, such as a physical ailment, discouragement, or depression, and never even be able to use the gift. But in all these instances love counts—and the more severe the trial or the problem the more significant love becomes.

Love is always eternally relevant—as opposed to prophecies, which shall be abolished, and gifts of tongues, which shall cease, and gifts of knowledge, which shall pass away.

In effect, Paul says that the one thing that stands high above everything else in life and in spiritual experience is love. He even said that if love is not in evidence in all the other areas of spiritual experience, then those areas are invalidated. Those are sobering words, but very important.

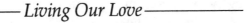
## Living Our Love

Have you seen gifts fall short of usefulness in your life or in someone else's? What happened? How were those gifts limited?

# Love is *the* fruit of the Spirit

> The fruit of the Spirit is love, joy, peace, patience,
> kindness, goodness, faithfulness, gentleness and
> self-control. Against such things there is no law.
> Those who belong to Christ Jesus have crucified the
> sinful nature, its passions, and desires. Since we live
> by the Spirit, let us keep in step with the Spirit. Let
> us not become conceited, provoking and envying
> each other. —*Galatians 5:22-25*

Though verses 22-23 form quite a long list, they are called the
"fruit of the Spirit." The word "fruit" is singular. You'd think
it would begin "The fruits of the Spirit *are*," but it doesn't.
There's a reason for this.

Sometimes we think of the various aspects of the spirit-
filled life as a supermarket of fruits. You walk along and, if
you're feeling very loving today, you pick up a loving orange;
if you're feeling very joyful today, you move across the aisle
to select a nice joyful plum. If you're not in the mood for
oranges today and only want plums, then you forget about
love for that day and just go for the joy.

Or perhaps you've got a particularly self-control/self-
disciplined personality, so you're really high on self-control
and you head straight for the pineapples of self-control every
time.

But we as Christians are not given this option. Not only are
we not given the freedom to pick and choose which of the
given "fruits"—as we tend to call them—of the Spirit we
want, neither are we given permission to "major" on our own
favorite fruit. So a person with a naturally loving disposition
can't go around telling people that "the fruit of the Spirit is
love," but reserve the freedom to be completely worried and

anxious all the time and never mention the fact that "peace" is also an aspect of the Spirit's fruit.

When we talk about the fruit of the Spirit, we're not discussing aspects or characteristics from which we can pick or choose, nor aspects of our personalities that come more naturally than others and so are to be concentrated upon.

No, the *fruit* of the Spirit is the culmination of God's many character traits growing and blooming in us. Fruit is the result of a growth process, and healthy growth brings a balance of all those things Galatians 5:22-23 names.

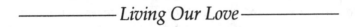

## *Living Our Love*

Spend some time in John 15:1-8.

# Love expresses the Christian's uniqueness

> By this all men will know that you are my disciples,
> if you love one another.　　　　　　　　—*John 13:35*

The Lord Jesus said clearly that the one thing that would give true viability and validity to the church of Jesus Christ in the eyes of a cynical world was that there would be something completely unique about Christians: the love they would demonstrate toward one another. There are few things more challenging than God's expectation of love in the community of believers—a love that permeates the lifestyle of those who follow Jesus.

The Bible shows that love comes in many different forms and on various levels, but what God and his people are interested in is love in its fullest, purest, and most magnificent sense. It is the love of God himself working itself out in our lives.

God intends that there be in us—our comings and goings, our words and actions—the unmistakable evidence that we belong to him. My life itself should be the most convincing argument that God has moved in. And the Bible says that this undeniable proof is love.

When a person comes to God on the basis of faith and receives what God offers in grace, he or she is made a new creation in Christ. As a result of being a new creation, that person will be motivated to a new lifestyle of thanksgiving, praise, and gratitude to God—and these qualities reveal love to a very ungrateful and unhappy world. The result is that the Christian looks quite unusual. When our aim, our pleasure, and our practice are love, we cannot help but stand out and make the world notice. This is how God intends the world to discover him—through the love of his children.

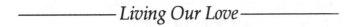

——————— *Living Our Love* ———————

What kinds of things clue you in to the fact that someone is a fellow believer in Jesus?

# Love's eternal significance

I will punish their sin with the rod, their iniquity
with flogging; but I will not take my love from him,
nor will I ever betray my faithfulness.   —*Psalm 89:32-33*

Right now we need faith, hope, and love. But we will not always need faith and hope. When we get to glory, the glory and the eternal nature of heaven will cancel the need for faith and hope. We will see God face to face! In such a state, faith and hope will no longer be necessary. But the very things that diminish the need for faith and hope are the very things that will stimulate our capacity for love.

In glory and eternity, we'll see the One who is love, who is the Source of all love. We'll see millions of people and created beings—together because of love. We'll be perfect in ourselves, and we'll love perfectly. So what's heaven going to be? An enormous experience of love.

In verse 10 of this chapter, Paul talks about "that which is perfect." The word that's used means "that which is the consummation of all things." The consummation of all things is going to come when God is seen to be God, when God is all in all. That's in eternity.

We've seen that God loves his Son, that he loves the world, and that he loves those who believe in his Son. And because he is agape love, he expects believers in his Son to love each other: "Love one another as I have loved you." This is the pattern. We are to love each other, fellow Christians in the body of Christ, even as the Father loves the Son and as the Son loves the Father.

How does the Father love the Son and the Son love the Father? Eternally. We're to love each other forever. So if you don't love somebody now, you'd better hurry up and get around to it because that's what it's going to be like for all eternity! If you're not into loving now, heaven could prove to be a disappointment!

——————— *Living Our Love* ———————

Pray the prayer on the next page.

# Prayer

Oh God, our heavenly Father, we know that one of the things that grieves you most is that the most beautiful thing you've given—love—has been so mistreated and so misunderstood in the world.

Lord, help us to understand the sheer perfection of your love in terms of its forgiveness and its sacrifice. Bear down upon our hearts with your Holy Spirit the truth of these things to such a degree that we might have an overwhelming desire to be imitators of God and walk in love, abstaining from its perversions and reproving them on every hand. Make us people who witness to the fact that God is love.

Lord, we have fallen in so many of these areas. Help us to know genuine repentance. Help us to know genuine confession and true cleansing and forgiveness. Lead us on from strength to strength that we might become people who know triumph in areas of previous disaster. It's beautiful to know that in the arms of Jesus and in the fellowship of his church, there is a place for the sinner to come and be cleansed—where they can experience the love of God through loving believers.

Deliver us from the deceptions so prevalent around us. Help us to see right through them and to choose love and to live lives dedicated to you and the coming of your kingdom on earth. In Christ's name, Amen.

PART 2

# The Qualities of Love

"We can learn so much about love by looking at the "love chapter," 1 Corinthians 13. When Paul wanted to paint a word portrait of Jesus, he wrote 1 Corinthians 13. The apostle thought about Jesus and described his character and his life by saying, 'Love is patient, love is kind . . . .' He could just as well have said Jesus is patient, Jesus is kind. He was overwhelmed with the possibility that our lives could become like Jesus'—that we could grow spiritually to reflect his likeness. 'And we, who with unveiled faces all reflect the Lord's glory, are being transformed into his likeness with ever-increasing glory, which comes from the Lord, who is the Spirit' (2 Corinthians 3:18).

"So, in describing the qualities of love, we shall look at this portrait of Jesus. Bit by bit, we'll fill in the colors, the substance and the shadows, the accents of Christ's love, and learn how the Spirit can change our unloveliness into his loveliness and our unloving ways into his loving attitudes."

—*Stuart and Jill Briscoe*

# "Charity suffers long"

> My dear brothers, take note of this: Everyone
> should be quick to listen, slow to speak and slow to
> become angry, for man's anger does not bring about
> the righteous life that God desires.      —*James 1:19-20*

Verse four of the King James Version of 1 Corinthians 13
begins, "Charity suffers long." That's another way of saying
that love is "longsuffering." The Greek word, *makrothumia*,
can also mean "long-wrathed" or "slow anger"; in other
words, it takes a long time to come to a boil.

You probably have some relationships in which it is quite
easy to "come to a boil." In any relationship where it is easy
to become angry, there is a lack of love. If it's easy to react to
a person in anger, then it's obvious that you're not primarily
concerned with that other person, but with what that person
is doing to you. In such a relationship, the best advice is to
stop focusing on that person and what that person is doing,
and start majoring on what God has commanded your attitude to be. Love will also be concerned to discover what could
be making a person behave in such a fashion. This helps us to
obey God's command that our attitude be "longsuffering."

Remembering the examples of longsuffering we have in
God our Creator and in Jesus the Son can make it easier to
cultivate this trait in ourselves. We see that God doesn't get
angry at us quickly:

> The LORD is compassionate and gracious, slow to
> anger, abounding in love.—*Psalm 103:8*

> The Lord is not slow in keeping his promise, as
> some understand slowness. He is patient with you,

not wanting anyone to perish, but everyone to come to repentance.—*2 Peter 3:9*

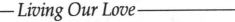
## *Living Our Love*

Memorize one of the above verses in whatever translation you like. At your next opportunity to "come to the boil," quote it silently to yourself, asking the Holy Spirit to make the verse real in your life right then.

# "Love is patient"

Love is patient, love is kind.     —*1 Corinthians 13:4*

Is patience the same as longsuffering? One advantage of so many translations of Scripture is that we sometimes discover different shades of the same thing. One aspect of longsuffering is that we don't anger easily; that's a specific kind of patience. But what else is involved in the phrase "love is patient"?

There is an element in patience called waiting. It's hard to wait and yet sometimes waiting does just as much to form the likeness of Jesus in us as suffering does. Think of the farmer. The farmer waits; he does his job; then he waits again. He knows that he must wait for sunshine, for rain, and just for time—for those plants to form and grow. If we are patient in the way a farmer is patient, then we will let God provide the sunshine and rain in our own lives and in other people's lives too. Sometimes there's nothing more we can do. That part of waiting is aptly described as *long*suffering. God knows how to wait, and we need to learn waiting from him.

Think of a romantic relationship. Perhaps you want a specific relationship to go somewhere, yet the other person needs more time. Maybe he or she is wounded and needs to finish healing from a past relationship. Maybe he or she has other areas of life to work out before committing to you. Love doesn't push. It's happy to give the other person space and time even though it's so hard to wait. Agape love describes how patient God is with us. We only have to look into our own hearts to realize that. And so God says to us, Now you be as patient with other people as I have been with you.

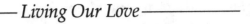 ——————— *Living Our Love* ———————

In what situation is it really hard for you to be patient right now? What kinds of sunshine and rain might this situation need before the change you want is able to happen? Ask the Lord to help you understand reasons for the waiting and to work in you the likeness of Christ because of it.

# Why must love suffer? In order that others may be helped.

> Surely he took up our infirmities
> and carried our sorrows,
> yet we considered him stricken by God,
> smitten by him, and afflicted.
> But he was pierced for our transgressions,
> he was crushed for our iniquities;
> the punishment that brought us peace was
>   upon him,
> and by his wounds we are healed.
>
> —*Isaiah 53:4-5*

Modern society tries to avoid suffering at all costs. Look at the euthanasia issue, or what we do to escape sorrows or trouble, through drugs or drink, work or play. We often forget that *it is part of the nature of life to suffer*. But it is also part of the nature of love. This is because loving someone else makes you vulnerable.

C.S. Lewis said, "Love anything and your heart will certainly be wrung and possibly be broken." The more we love the more we can expect to suffer. Why does God allow suffering? Because he encourages loving, and suffering is part of loving. Much of suffering is experienced in relationships. And since relationships incorporate vulnerability, we can expect to suffer. We will hurt, too, when people we love hurt. We will endure pain, anxiety, and depression along with them. But when they see us hurting with them, it can help to alleviate their distress.

Picture in your mind's eye a suffering God. When we see God in Christ suffering on Calvary for our sakes—for our healing and help—then we are encouraged to bear our own pain, in order to better understand and alleviate the suffering of others.

## Living Our Love

Meditate on the verses from Isaiah. Then think of the people in your life—parents, friends, children—who are suffering. Allow these thoughts and the testimony of God's Word to strengthen your resolve to "weep with those who weep" and help them through their suffering.

# "Love is kind"

> Those who are kind reward themselves, but the
> cruel do themselves harm. —*Proverbs 11:17* (NRSV)

Some people are naturally more kind than others. It's often a matter of personality. However, whatever your personality might be, the principle remains: love always operates toward the other person in terms of kindness.

The Greek word for "kind" is *chrestos*. In the early days of Christianity, Christians were known as followers of "Christos." Some people confused the two words and thought they were followers of kindness: in a sense, they were!

What is kindness? The word is sometimes translated as "gentleness," sometimes as "goodness," and on one occasion as "easy," as in Jesus' description of his yoke which the people were to take upon them (Matthew 11:30). Kindness is "gentle." Sometimes we put heavy expectations on people that feels like a "yoke" to them—a heavy load. We need to be merciful, not cruel and heartless when dealing with another person, especially if we are in authority. Even when we have a valid reason to lay something "heavy" on someone, the way we do it can invalidate the whole interaction, if we are not kind or considerate.

Jesus says, "The yoke I would have you take on yourself is perfectly valid, but the way I'll lay it on you will feel easy, kind, and gentle. That is because I have a great concern for you. After all, love is kind. I am love!"

If you find yourself in a position of leadership and authority and you are called upon as part of your position to "lay" things on other people, then you must carefully analyze the way you're doing it. Are you allowing for kindness, gentleness, a margin for error, and flexibility? If not, you run the risk of being too authoritarian and lacking in love.

This is a problem some husbands have to deal with. They receive so much teaching and emphasis on a wife's submission that they tend to gloss over the clear scriptural teaching that they should first be submitting to one another as well. Harsh men can lay things on their wives in an unloving way. We can also be harsh with our children or with coworkers. Simple kindness eliminates so much that is bad in relationships; it's much more likely to be effective than harshness. We must remember that kindness is always a part of agape love—and therefore required of us by God.

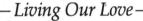

### ———————— *Living Our Love* ————————

Think of something you need to "lay" on another person—a job that needs to be done, a correction that needs to be made, a reprimand, or a demand for more time or better work. Now put yourself in the other person's place and imagine how you would like this thing to be "laid" on you. What words would you want the person to use? What manner of speaking and presenting the information would make it easier for you to accept what's being said and asked of you? What, on the other hand, would put you on the defensive, hurt you, or make you angry? As you explore the other person's position, plan specifically how you are going to approach him or her in kindness.

# "Love is not envious"

> We lived in malice and envy, being hated and
> hating one another. But when the kindness and love
> of God our Savior appeared, he saved us . . . I want
> you to stress these things, so that those who have
> trusted God may be careful to devote themselves to
> doing what is good.                               —*Titus 3:3-5, 8*

Love does not envy. The Greek word is *zelos*, from which we
get the English word *zeal*. James uses it to talk about people
who are driven by selfish ambition to acquire things (James
3:14-16).

There's no question that one of the great motivating forces
of all individuals and the driving dynamic force behind our
contemporary economy is the desire to acquire. We are naturally motivated to acquire things but are artificially stimulated to get more things. Then we're caught up in an economic
rat race. This stimulation of people's desire to have and have
and have can be dangerous.

Very often the desire to acquire is at the expense of somebody else. The more I desire to have at the expense of another
person, the more I know that I do not love that person.

In the Ten Commandments, envy is called *coveting*. "You
shall not covet your neighbor's house, your neighbor's wife,
your neighbor's maidservants, ox, donkey." Some people say
that when you get to the situation where you say, "I want what
you've got," you are envious. But when you add, "and I don't
want you to have it, either," you're into jealousy—and jealousy is into you. If God does not deal with that attitude in our
lives, then it may harden into the very jealousy that we see
causing all sorts of injury and abuse.

An excellent example of this kind of envy and jealousy is King Saul, who knew that God had chosen David to take the throne after him (1 Samuel 18-19). Saul's jealousy turned him murderous; he tried to kill David and hunted him for months.

Now Saul had a son, Jonathan, who would, logically, follow Saul as King of Israel. However, Jonathan knew that God had chosen David for that role. One would think that Jonathan would be even more jealous than Saul. But Jonathan loved David (1 Samuel 20) and accepted God's plan. Therefore jealousy did not get the upper hand in Jonathan's life; in fact, he helped to save David's life from Saul.

The only thing that can overcome covetousness, envy, and jealousy is love. Love can overcome jealousy when we open ourselves up, when we repent of what we see in ourselves that we know should have no place in our lives. We need to say, "God, I am sorry. I am sick of it. Forgive me." And then we need to open ourselves up to the Holy Spirit, and he will begin to work graciously in our attitude.

Love doesn't envy because love is always thinking of the other person's well-being. In fact, love—true love—will rejoice in the other person's blessings.

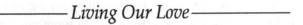

## ——————— *Living Our Love* ———————

Who are you most likely to be jealous or envious of? Why? Pray very specifically for that person or those persons, and thank God for the blessings he has placed in their lives. Ask God to help them with the difficult parts of their lives, too.

# "Love does not boast"

> "Let not the wise man boast of his wisdom or the
> strong man boast of his strength or the rich man
> boast of his riches, but let him who boasts boast
> about this: that he understands and knows me, that
> I am the LORD, who exercises kindness, justice and
> righteousness on earth, for in these I delight,"
> declares the LORD.                    —*Jeremiah 9:23-24*

"Charity vaunteth not itself" is the King James translation
of 1 Corinthians 13:4. That sounds good and poetic, but what
does it mean? It means "love is not boastful."

This word is not used in any other New Testament context.
But it was a word particularly apropos to the Corinthians,
who tended to boast. They were so wrapped up in what they
had and in what they'd done and in what they were going to
do that they couldn't care less about anyone else. So all the
time they were boasting with billowing words about all their
achievements, other people didn't matter to them.

It's sometimes difficult to avoid boasting in the church of
Jesus Christ, too, because the church is often very pragmatic.
We may have decided how to evaluate whether a church is
successful. For example, very often we measure a church's
success on the basis of numbers. Pastors' conversations often
revolve around numbers and the growth of membership.
Juan Carlos Ortiz, a pastor, illumines this wrong perception
of success. He says that he was very proud that the congrega-
tion he pastored was growing until he passed a cemetery one
day and noticed that *it*, too, was growing. He pointed out that
sometimes growth is just fat! The problem is that we can be
so caught up with the things we are doing and never be truly
interested in people. And that's unloving.

So "love vaunteth not itself, is not puffed up." The Greek word connotes the idea of an inflated windbag. It describes pride perfectly. Somebody who "vaunts" himself is too full of his own importance, always blowing off at the mouth. If we achieve anything at all in life worth talking about, it is far better to let another praise us for it.

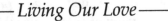

## ———— *Living Our Love* ————

Make a list of what you consider to be your best achievements. Now take a good look at what you've written down. Is it a list of things you've done that benefited your self-esteem, like completing a tough graduate course, losing twenty pounds, creating something new that others could admire? How many of your best achievements involved active relationship with others? If your list doesn't comply with God's idea of achievements, then come up with some new types of things to achieve, and take steps to begin.

# "Love is not puffed up"

> Knowledge puffs up, but love builds up.
>
> —*1 Corinthians 8:1*

"Puffed up" is an expression Paul used to describe the Corinthians because one of their biggest problems was that they had an inflated view of themselves. He told them that they were arrogant and proud—and that is the exact opposite of love.

No one can be lovingly proud or proud of being loving. Pride is basically the exaltation of self over another. Sometimes we're proud of our children's accomplishments—mostly because that puts our kids ahead of other kids. Sometimes we're proud of what our church has accomplished—mostly because our church is doing something another church isn't doing. We tend to be proud of our business—mostly because our business got ahead of the other businesses. Pride is primarily directed at what I have done in contrast to what others have done. Pride says, "I'm much more interested in myself than in you, especially if I can look better at your expense." That's a flat contradiction of the whole concept of love.

Love, of course, isn't proud. People who love don't see themselves as more important or more gifted or more loving than anyone else. In fact, people who love don't spend a lot of time or energy thinking about themselves at all. They merely spend time "doing for others," not worrying about where the profit is for them. They realize that God, the ultimate Love, is in charge of all things, and that he will honor their humble attitudes toward themselves and others.

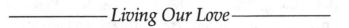

## Living Our Love

Brainstorm some things you could do for others around you. Then do something each day this week to demonstrate that other people are more important than you are.

# Love is *not* a crocodile!

> Can you pull in the leviathan with a fishhook or tie down his tongue with a rope? . . . If you lay a hand on him, you will remember the struggle and never do it again! Any hope of subduing him is false; the mere sight of him is overpowering. . . . His snorting throws out flashes of light . . . firebrands stream from his mouth; the folds of his flesh are tightly joined; they are firm and immovable. His chest is hard as rock, hard as a lower millstone. When he rises up, the mighty are terrified. . . . He makes the depths churn like a boiling cauldron and stirs up the sea like a pot of ointment. Behind him he leaves a glistening wake. . . . He looks down on all that are haughty; he is king over all that are proud.
>
> —*selections from Job 41*

You've probably noticed that no crocodiles turn up *anywhere* in 1 Corinthians! But there were plenty of proud people, and the crocodile is king of the proud. This dramatic picture is well worth our consideration. There may be a crocodile of pride lurking in the swamp of our lives. The crocodile says, "I am a king, a monarch." It's a forceful, arrogant creature. Everybody is afraid of it.

Pride coerces. Love doesn't coerce. Love pleads; love discusses. But the crocodile doesn't bother pleading or discussing. This creature of pride is intimidating, impossible for others to manage or even try to handle. Remember when the devil told Jesus he could have all the kingdoms of the world? Satan was trying to appeal to pride. But Jesus, even though he was King, said all along that he didn't come to throw his weight around, but to serve. He refused to be intimidated, and he despised intimidation. He says to us, "I won't force you to serve me out of fear. You can serve me if you like, but only because you like. Only if you want to, and only if you will."

Verse 18 says, "the light plays on the crocodile's snorting snout." Verse 19 says, "sparks fly out"; then verse 20 talks of "steam, seething water, and boiling pots." All these word pictures lead us to believe that the terrible creature needs his tongue tied securely down with a string. Don't we all know people like this? Aren't we like this ourselves? Verse 25 says there will be a swirl in the water when the crocodile comes up, and he will terrify strong men. When you see a proud man coming, you usually don't want to be around him. A woman who loves to brag usually doesn't have too many friends. We fear their constant company.

Have you ever been with someone who will never admit to another point of view? They won't even let it into their mind for a moment. They've got all their armor plating on. They never admit they're wrong. Maybe we're guilty of that. *It has to be the other person who's wrong; it couldn't possibly be me,* we say to ourselves. Verse 22, "strength is seated in his neck," is a poignant phrase. The crocodile is not going to bow his neck to anyone. And in verse 24, "his heart is stout as a millstone." Watch for the crocodile of pride rearing his ugly head in you, and make an effort to change now—before pride hardens your heart.

## ——————— *Living Our Love* ———————

Spend some time in Job 41, exploring pride and asking God to help you understand the opposite of pride: love.

# "Love is not rude"

Love has good manners and does not pursue selfish advantage. —*1 Corinthians 13:5 (PHILLIPS)*

"Charity doth not behave itself unseemly" (KJV). What does that mean? To behave oneself unseemly was something that Paul was often concerned about throughout his writing in the New Testament.

Paul taught that love must always demonstrate the highest ethical standards. Love does not misbehave sexually. Love does not misbehave politically. Love does not misbehave socially in any way. Love has a high regard for that which is ethically correct and of the highest standard in the eyes of God. If your ethical standards are slipping, whether in accountability in your business or even in your manner to others while waiting in line, you can be sure you're not acting in love.

This phrase, "love is not rude," carries a tremendous message for us today, if only we will hear it. We are becoming amoral in areas political, sexual, social, and financial. *The more amoral we become, the less loving we become.* Scripture says firmly that love will always be of the highest ethical caliber.

Let's think about a simple thing—like standing in line. Love is courteous, never pushy. It doesn't push to the front of the line and say, "Me first!" Love doesn't do that because love has good manners. And Christian believers should exhibit the charm of Jesus himself, who never forced his way upon us, even though he knew his way could make our way so much more pleasant and fulfilling. In fact, the Scriptures say that he stands at the door and knocks (Revelation 3:20). He doesn't barge into our hearts and say, "You need me and you'd better let me in." He says, "Please, may I come in?" What grace, what charm—what love.

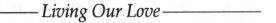

## Living Our Love

Take note of the way in which others treat you rudely this week. Turn that around and ask yourself when you have acted this way, and under what circumstances. What actions and words of others are offensive to you? Ask the Holy Spirit to alert you when *you* are behaving in a similar way.

# "Love is not self-seeking"

> I hope in the Lord Jesus to send Timothy to you
> soon, that I also may be cheered when I receive
> news about you. I have no one else like him who
> takes a genuine interest in your welfare. For
> everyone looks out for his own interests, not those
> of Jesus Christ. —*Philippians 2:19-21*

In the above Scripture passage, Paul is heartbroken. After all his work with so many disciples, teaching them, training them, praying with them, encouraging them, it seems that only Timothy can be trusted to look out for the interests of others more than those of himself. Others insisted on staying where they were, occupying themselves with their own tasks and priorities. They didn't want to get involved; they were too wrapped up and only interested in themselves. Poor Paul! He was training disciples and also experiencing tremendous frustration because they only wanted to "seek their own."

In 1 Corinthians 13:5, Paul explains that those who "seek their own" do not love people. One of the characteristics of love is a desire and attitude that is not primarily concerned with how it's going to affect oneself but more with what to do in Christ's name for someone else.

Looking out for "number one" comes so naturally. But God's love isn't natural; it doesn't seek its own way. As we grow up spiritually, agape love should rule over the natural urge to be so selfish. But for the time being, many of us are children—and we exhibit childish behavior as believers. May we instead grow up into the image of Christ, adulthood, and spiritual maturity.

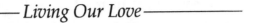

## *Living Our Love*

You've probably daydreamed about the things you would like to do with your life—spiritual gifts you'd like to develop, natural talents you'd like to use, milestones you'd like to pass. Think of a fellow believer you know fairly well. Daydream about what God could do with *that* life. Write out the things you envision for a person with his or her personality and gifts. When you've dreamed and prayed over that person, make a date to share your thoughts. This doesn't mean that you are dictating the person's future, only that you're helping him or her dream toward God's kind of gifts and goals.

# "Love is not easily angered"

A hot-tempered man stirs up dissension, but a
patient man calms a quarrel.          —*Proverbs 15:18*

We get uncomfortable when we're told we shouldn't have a temper, don't we? The original Greek of this 1 Corinthians 13 phrase does not include that cushion word "easily." And that makes it even harder to take.

I have been angered ("provoked" in KJV), and friends have said, "Well, you tried. You were patient for a long time. Sure, you blew it in the end, but you held out a long time before giving in to the provocation." That makes me feel good, but the truth is that *any* time I am provoked I am not acting in love. Being provoked shows a mindset of being more concerned about what a person is doing to me than with being concerned for what I should be doing for that person.

That word *angered* or *provoked* could be literally translated "sharpened." Love is not easily sharpened—or, love doesn't get needled! When you get hypersensitive with another person and react, you are not loving.

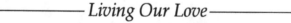

——————— *Living Our Love* ———————

Unfortunately, there's no way to improve in this area—no way to practice this character quality—without someone provoking us! You can ask yourself, however, what it is that "pushes your buttons" in some situations and makes you angry so easily. Does it happen when you already feel threatened or belittled? Does it happen only with certain people whom you haven't developed a liking for? Once you search yourself for clues, you can begin to work on not being so sensitive.

# "Love keeps no record of wrongs"

I, even I, am he who blots out your transgressions,
for my own sake, and remembers your sins no more.

—Isaiah 43:25

I once visited a primitive tribe in South America. Noticing odd objects hanging from the ceilings in their huts, I asked about them. The people explained: "We have many enemies. Each time someone hurts us, we hang up a remembrance of it. Each time someone does us wrong, does us evil, says something about us, to make sure we never forget we hang a symbol of their action up there" (pointing to the different objects)—"that's what he did, and that's what she did, and that's what they did twenty years ago."

We are tempted to think, *how primitive!* Primitive nothing! Some of our minds are just like that. We hang all sorts of remembrances of what "he did to me twenty years ago" and "what she did ten years ago" and "what he did last week"— all over our minds in case we forget. Yet real love doesn't do that, for love has a renewed mind and refuses to keep score. If God has forgiven these people we must forgive them, too. What God has forgotten we have no right to remember.

It is no simple matter to let go of past hurts. The reason it's so difficult is that we've been *hurt*. A scratch will heal up and disappear, and we forget about it. But a major injury can take months, even years, to heal completely. Sometimes we can't just dismiss it and get on with life. The hurts inflicted on us by others fall into different categories—some important categories and others less important. Someone forgetting to pick you up for an appointment—well, it's irritating, but you get over it in a few hours. Someone you think of as a friend accusing you of being dishonest—now that's a major injury. Only God's love can heal something like that.

Sometimes we can't see any good reason for such an excruciating hurt occurring. But, if nothing else, deep wounds force us to depend more on God's love and grace than anything else. Some things are just impossible to forgive—they're so malicious. And if they happen between friends or within the family they are ten times worse, because we've already invested so much and made ourselves so vulnerable. But God tells us to forgive, just as he has forgiven our malice, hatred, selfishness, pettiness, immorality, etc. We can only forgive with the love God gives to us, the love that must be transplanted and grow inside us.

So, don't be surprised when forgiveness is difficult, even impossible. Just take it as a cue to pray more desperately for God to do the forgiving for you, by his love in you reaching to others—especially those who've been so hurtful.

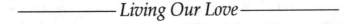

## Living Our Love

Pray for specific people who have hurt you in ways that are hard to forgive.

# Love doesn't assume the worst in people

> You, then, why do you judge your brother? Or why
> do you look down on your brother? For we will all
> stand before God's judgment seat.      —*Romans 14:10*

We find in 1 Corinthians 13:5 of the King James version that love "thinks no evil." This immediately makes you remember those three monkeys—hear no evil (with paws over its ears), see no evil (with paws over its eyes), and speak no evil (paws over its mouth). You can imagine a fourth: think no evil, with paws holding the head. But the translation "think no evil" does not do full justice to what Paul wrote.

The actual Greek word he used incorporates the idea of "logic," "reason," "reckon," or "calculate." When someone does something to hurt us or bother us, we tend to keep careful accounts. "I'll never forgive you for that," we promise. Years later, when we find ourselves in terrible problems and we wonder how it came about, a skilled psychologist might take us back to that awful point where we calculatedly kept account of someone's wrongs. This evil thinking has taken its toll on our health, our mental well-being, and our relationships.

Love never says, "I'll never forgive you for that." And it doesn't keep records.

Love also does not look at what others are saying and attribute (or calculate) evil motives to them. In other words, *love doesn't think the worst* about someone.

There is no lower blow than to attribute a bad motive to someone who is acting in good faith with loving intentions. Yet it is a common practice in our dog-eat-dog society. We can be so cynical and harsh and unloving in our attitudes toward people that our instant reflex is to think the worst of them.

When you go in with accusations about a person's motives, you have left love behind. *Love always gives a person the benefit of the doubt.* That doesn't mean you can't communicate to another person, in love, that you think his actions were wrong or hurtful. But love can't go further than that and accuse another of malice or hurtful *intent.* I don't have the power or the wisdom to truly know what is going on inside others' minds and hearts. To assume that I know another person's motives is utterly arrogant on my part.

Love does not attribute evil motives. Love does not keep account of wrongs. Love does not calculate evil. If this principle were really put into action, we could probably go ahead and close down the majority of marriage counseling clinics. And fewer people would have to cross the street in order to avoid someone else!

────────── *Living Our Love* ──────────

Imagine a scenario in which you believe someone has wronged you (maybe you don't have to imagine at all!). Now think of all the possible causes for that person's words or actions, *excluding* the possibility that this person was intentionally trying to hurt you. What are some factors in daily life that can cause us to wrong others, even though we're not out to hurt anyone? To what factors are you particularly vulnerable? Stress at work? Fatigue? A suspicious mind? Anger at something completely unrelated? Ask the Holy Spirit to search your heart, giving you keys to overcome your own tendency to hurt others. Ask also for help in refraining from attributing evil motives to others when they hurt you.

# Love doesn't enjoy bad news

> Jesus answered, "Do you think that these Galileans
> were worse sinners than all the other Galileans
> because they suffered in this way? I tell you, no! But
> unless you repent, you too will all perish. Or those
> eighteen who died when the tower in Siloam fell on
> them—do you think they were more guilty than all
> the others living in Jerusalem? I tell you, no! But
> unless you repent, you too will all perish."
>
> —*Luke 13:2-5*

"Love does not delight in evil" (1 Corinthians 13:6). We are inclined to dismiss this kind of statement. After all, who would take delight in evil? Yet sometimes we actually feel gratified when bad things happen—to someone else, of course.

For instance, let's say someone else got your place as wide receiver on the football team, and you've been feeling terrible about it. The day of the big game dawns, and it's pouring rain. You go to the field, prepared to sit the bench while the others play in the thick mud. Then the first-string quarterback breaks his hand. You might look out at the wide receiver playing your position and think, *Pouring rain, thick mud, and a replacement quarterback—you're going to have a stinker of a game, and I'm going to enjoy every minute of it!*

We do rejoice in a bitter sort of way over the misfortune in others' lives. Sometimes it's because we think they deserve it. Don't we enjoy hearing about a crooked politician who gets himself into a mess? Seeing investigative reporters put guilty people on the spot and watching them squirm on camera? We love it, don't we? Sometimes bad things happening to other people makes us look better than them. We obviously are doing something right, or else the same misfortunes would befall us, wouldn't they? That's the attitude Jesus addressed in the passage above.

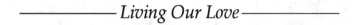

## Living Our Love

The next time someone you dislike gets "what they deserve," or has something bad happen, don't gloat secretly. Instead, pray for him or her.

# Love doesn't gossip

> For I am afraid that when I come I may not find you
> as I want you to be . . . I fear that there may be
> quarreling, jealousy, outbursts of anger, factions,
> slander, gossip, arrogance and disorder.
>
> —*2 Corinthians 12:20*

We can't talk about rejoicing in evil without dealing with the area of gossip because as we rejoice in the troubles of another person, we're bound to talk about it. But when the Bible says we're not to rejoice in others' iniquity, that includes being quiet about it. Gossip may be enjoyed vicariously. When people take great delight in talking about someone else's misbehavior, they are probably deriving a secret thrill from something they themselves would be afraid to do openly.

We've made a national business of gossip. Look at the talk shows that thrive on people spilling their own guts and then exposing the vice in the lives of others. At certain times of the day, that's all you can find on the television. You flip from channel to channel, and all you find is the corporate enjoyment of evil. It seems to be the fashionable thing to do. "Don't hold back. Be brutally honest. The more outrageous, the better."

Yes, love is honest. But love is slow to expose. In love we must ask ourselves, "Will exposure aid in the healing and repenting process? Will exposure help or hinder? Will it wound?" And even when love does expose, it gets no pleasure from it—because love does not delight in evil.

Sometimes when people come to Christ they feel the need to share what's happening in their lives. But I have seen occasions when most inappropriate things were "shared." When love is in control, we know that some things we share will not help. Discretion is needed because the danger of being totally open is that we don't learn what is appropriate to share, and what is not. The youngest son of Noah told a great story about his father's alcohol problem. His older brothers were more loving—they covered his shame with a blanket.

Then there's the prayer meeting. Have you ever been in a prayer meeting with Little Miss Let-me-tell-you-all-that-I-can't-tell-you-if-I-have-my-eyes-open? Her intentions may be impeccable, but her discretion is suspect. Her prayers border on gossip. She shuts her eyes and prays, "Oh God, we pray for little Ann. She's finding such a struggle being tempted by that married man." Of course everyone's interested to hear the rest of *that* story. She could just as easily, and rightfully, pray, "Lord, Ann's really having a tough time; she's got a big problem. We'd like to support her because she's a new Christian." God will hear that prayer and answer it. He knows what's happening to Ann and he not only cares but wants us to care, too. Everybody else doesn't have to know the gory details. Love doesn't gossip. Love knows when exposure hurts, not helps.

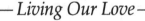

## Living Our Love

Make a point this week *not* to talk about bad news— the crooked bigshots getting exposed, the latest murderer or rapist, the newest "dirt" at church. Make an agreement with yourself (and maybe with someone else) to refrain from being part of these kinds of conversation.

# "Love rejoices in the truth"

> I have no greater joy than to hear that my children
> are walking in the truth.                          —*3 John 1:4*

Love doesn't delight in evil. That's the negative aspect. But it rejoices in the truth. That's positive. Love looks for something that's good. Love eagerly looks past a person's sin to his potential, and earnestly rejoices in evidence of blessing in another's life.

That's why Love looked at Peter one day and said, Simon, you shall be Peter. That's why Love looked down from heaven one day and said, Saul, you shall be Paul. That's why Love looked down at Jacob one day and said, Jacob, you shall be Israel. Love rejoices in the potential one sees and doesn't put emphasis on the present imperfections. And that's what the mindset of the Spirit of God can do for us. Wouldn't it be marvelous if we all started living lives like this? It's possible; it's within reach.

We can rejoice in the truth more easily when we take a truthful look at ourselves. We can truthfully say, "I'm quick to anger. I love to gossip. I delight in evil. I do not rejoice in the truth. I'm a mess. Yet I'm a person who professes to know Christ. And bit by bit and day by day and stage by stage, I'm coming to the point where I'm sick of myself. I'm getting closer to true agape love. I know that I am not what I want to be, but I'm moving toward it steadily by God's grace." Why not look with that much charity on other people instead of tending to see their obvious faults and failings? We forget that they have the capability to move toward the Lord, too.

Have you noticed how a politician running for office will maximize his opponent's faults and failings and minimize his own, while maximizing his own successes and minimizing those of his opponent? This may be normal in political life, but it has no place in spiritual life. Love is always thrilled when the right thing happens. This doesn't necessarily come naturally. Just because the right thing happens doesn't mean that we're getting what we want. We don't always want what's right—and the right thing for us sometimes is not to get what we want while others get what they long for. Love rejoices even when I feel needy and neglected and my brother seems to have fallen into fantastic blessing.

Love is interested in undergirding the right, no matter where I figure in the picture. Love always has a fine sense of that which is right and is committed to seeing it happen.

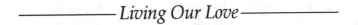

## *Living Our Love*

During prayer time, visualize and pray for the potential of someone you don't like very well.

# "Love bears all things"

> Do not let any unwholesome talk come out of your
> mouths, but only what is helpful for building others
> up according to their needs, that it may benefit
> those who listen. —*Ephesians 4:29*

The Greek word translated "bears" is *stego*. It was only used on a couple of occasions in the Bible, but it was used in more than one way in common Greek. An understanding of how the word was used in Paul's day helps us to better understand why he chose it for this passage.

To bear all things means to cover or conceal a secret matter. This goes right along with not rejoicing in evil, in not enjoying bad news. It also fits perfectly with love not keeping records of how it's been wronged.

Love also covers or conceals sins—other people's sins. The Greek meaning is that we "cover with silence." It means that love has such a respect for the real value of that person that love won't be dragging the skeleton out of the closet all the time. He won't be rejoicing in gossip. Keep in mind that sin grieves—hurts—God. And if you love God, you don't want to be talking about things that grieve him all the time. Love doesn't dwell on the sins of others. In this way, love covers over or "bears" the ugliness in others' lives.

"When I was a child, I spoke as a child," said Paul. Part of childhood is tattling—making sure that others know all the bad things that so-and-so is doing. It's a trait we have to discipline out of children. One of the ways we do this is to say, No, I don't want to know what so-and-so is doing. And then when they've left the room, you find out for yourself who's doing what. But we don't want our children to grow up to be tattle-tales.

But some people never grow up. They tattle all their lives. They do a good bit of their tattling in the church of Jesus Christ. When you love someone, and that person falls on hard times, you don't rejoice in the fact and spread it around. Instead, you cover and protect the whole situation lovingly.

Love is durable, able to cope. *Stego* can also mean "to protect by covering" or "to seal" as if making a ship water-tight. The idea is that love can bear a heavy load without distributing it all over the place. It keeps its mouth shut. In professional counseling there is a confidentiality factor where the counselor may not divulge information about the counse-lee without his or her permission. Something similar, on a voluntary basis, is evidence of love.

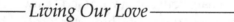 ——————— *Living Our Love* ———————

What situations are the most difficult to keep quiet about? How can you discourage unedifying discussions that take place around you?

# Love is a blanket

> Above all, love each other deeply, because love
> covers over a multitude of sins.       —*1 Peter 4:8*

Another meaning of this Greek word for "bears" has to do with blanketing something. It means that love runs around and throws itself over other people's faults like a great big heavenly blanket. So we can run around and throw ourselves over (covering up) other people's faults and feelings.

But the role model is God. He keeps confidences, all confidences; your secrets are safe with him. Maybe there's nobody else you could ever share your secret with. You know why it's so safe to share your secret with God? However bad, however black, however desperate, however terrible, horrible, dreadful, frightening, he will keep your confidence.

The Trinity doesn't sit around gossiping about us, even with all the information God the Father, God the Son, and God the Holy Spirit have about each of us. Moment by moment, our faults and sins and failures are coming to the attention of the Trinity. I can imagine them looking down and saying to each other—"What a mess. Just look at those people running around down there. Look at the sin. And that Jill Briscoe—she's the worst of the lot of them. What are we going to do about her? We've got to take our great big heavenly blanket of love and go down and cover the mess up!" That's what love did and does. Love came down to the cross of Christ and became a propitiation—a covering, a blanket—for our sins. "Blessed is he whose transgressions are forgiven, whose sins are covered," Psalm 32:1 says. And so, as he covered our sins, we—with his love—can cover the sins of others.

———————— *Living Our Love* ————————

Think of a situation close to you that requires the "heavenly blanket" treatment. In what practical way can you cover that person with love—throw your forgiveness over them?

# Love can keep a secret

Carry each others' burdens, and in this way you
will fulfill the law of Christ.          —*Galatians 6:2*

The word *stego* also conveyed the picture of a tower, a reinforced strong place. It didn't matter how many people as-
saulted it; it was never taken. This strong place was a tower
that was reinforced so that, when everything else in the city
had fallen during the assault, the tower was still standing.

You know, it's very tempting in Christian circles to say, "I
just want to share something with you. Somebody's told me
something, and it's a serious matter." Maybe it is a serious
matter, and you just want to share it so someone else can bear
it as well, but love doesn't do that—not unless it's very
clearly directed to. Love is reinforced with astute silence.
Love is like a tower.

Can you keep that confidence? Is their secret safe with you?

That's something I (Jill) admire about Stuart. There are
many, many things day in and day out he has to keep from
everybody—including me, his children, and his pastoral
friends. People have told him secret things, and they must
know their secrets are safe with him. Now you may think that,
of course, a *pastor* must be trustworthy in this way. (Unfortunately, not all pastors are.) But this characteristic should be
part of *every* believer's makeup, for love bears all things. So
whether you're a pastor or a housewife, you've got to be the
sort of person who keeps a secret safe.

*Stego* also connoted a pillar that carried a heavy roof, so an
army could march over it. Are you the sort of person who is
so strong that even though an army is going to march over
you, you're going to carry that secret safely? It doesn't matter
what weight it puts on you. Sometimes sharing people's

problems does mean, quite literally, to carry something heavy—the weight of someone else's sin.

This aspect of loving scares some people off from really living the Christian life. They think, *I don't want to grow up spiritually because I might have to be an encourager, a counselor. And if I become an encourager or a counselor, I'm going to have to bear other people's secrets. And I can't do that because I've got enough problems of my own.* So we prevent ourselves from going on to serve others in love. Yet love bears all things.

Some time ago I (Jill) was facing some serious surgery. I knew for six weeks that I would have to have it done. It was a heavy thing for me to bear. And for many reasons, I couldn't share it. But I did share it with about ten people. Ten people knew about that thing for six weeks. And you know, I'm constantly thankful to those people, so proud of their maturity. They were as watertight as a ship; the information never leaked out. I knew that I could trust them. That was a tremendous thing for me to see the maturity of people who carried the weight for me, for I needed that. And at the same time they bore my burden; they kept the confidence; they demonstrated love at its highest. And that's what we have to do for other people.

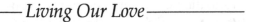 *Living Our Love*

Recall a time when someone helped you carry a burden. How did they do that? How can you carry someone else's burden in this way?

# "Love always trusts"

[Love] always protects, always trusts, always hopes,
always perseveres.                    —*1 Corinthians 13:7*

The King James Version translates the phrase "always trusts" as "believes all things." That does not mean that love is gullible! An unbeliever reading this might say, "Those dumb Christians—they'll believe any old thing!" That's not what it is saying at all. The meaning is that love is always prepared to retain faith in a person, because *love never believes that anyone is beyond redemption.*

Love doesn't cut someone off finally and irrevocably. Love always maintains faith for something greater than is in evidence at present.

Compare two completely different scenarios. In the first, the son comes to his father and says, "Dad, you drive me up the wall, and I see absolutely no way that I can survive your untender care."

And the father says, "Let me tell you, son, the sooner you get out of this house, the sooner I'll be pleased. I prefer your room to your company."

That situation is not as uncommon as you think. In a loving situation the son might come to his dad and say, "Dad, I don't really know what it is about you and about me that we rub each other the wrong way. But I honestly believe it can be resolved. I'm going to work on it."

Or in a marriage. A woman might say, "I've had it up to here, and I'm going home to mother!" instead of saying, "I've had it up to here, but it's not over my head yet! I honestly believe that there is hope for us." That's love.

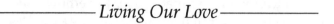

## Living Our Love

Is there some relationship in which you are having a difficult time with trust? What kinds of statements are you tempted to say about this person ("He'll never change." "She's just like her mother, so I might as well give up now." "He's always been like that; why expect improvement?")? What kinds of statements would love's kind of trust help you to make?

# Love keeps hoping

May the God of hope fill you with all joy and peace as you trust in him, so that you may overflow with hope by the power of the Holy Spirit.   —*Romans 15:13*

I heard a story once about somebody going to the Matterhorn. They'd waited a long time to go to Switzerland to see it. And when they got there the day was terrible; it was like England—just fog, fog, fog. They couldn't see a thing. Incredibly, they said, "I don't believe there's a Matterhorn. I can't see it, so I don't believe it's there." It was there, of course, but they couldn't see it because it was shrouded in fog.

What an allegory of a seemingly hopeless situation. The Matterhorn is there. You just can't see it because you're immersed in the fog.

Hope is for just this kind of situation; it sees through the fog to the reality beyond. Love keeps hoping. It refuses to think failure is final because human failure is never final. Hope hangs on for the future. Abraham is a perfect example. One day he came to his wife and said, "Sarah, we're going to have a baby." "A what?" squealed his wife. How ridiculous it was. And you know what it says in the Bible about Abraham? When hope was gone he hoped on in faith.

That's what we've got to do. When we can't see all the marvelous things we're praying will happen, we've got to hope on in faith.

In this way—the way of hope—love is optimistic. This is not the naive optimism of "I hope everything is going to work out all right . . . ," but a certainty based on fact—the fact of God's love toward us.

I (Jill) often say to Stuart that I am going to put on his tombstone: "Here lies Stuart Briscoe. He never anticipated any major problem!" I guess he's a born optimist. But that's not exactly the kind of optimism that Paul is describing in 1 Corinthians. This is not an optimism born of personality but rather of faith.

Love is prepared to hope and trust and believe and go on refusing to accept failure as final. This is a kind of love that never gives up.

Love is optimistic. Love is tenacious. It keeps hoping.

## Living Our Love

Is there an area of your life that seems hopeless? Turn it over to Christ and say, "I don't have any hope left; it's up to you, Lord, to give me the faith I need to carry on."

# John Mark and Barnabas

> We who are strong ought to bear with the failings of
> the weak and not to please ourselves. Each of us
> should please his neighbor for his good, to build
> him up. —*Romans 15:1-2*

A wonderful real-life story of love's principles in ministry is
that of Barnabas and John Mark. Here was John Mark—a
young man who made an absolute mess of his Christian walk.
It began when he wanted to follow Christ. One night he heard
that Jesus was somewhere near the Garden of Gethsemane.
Apparently John Mark had already gone to bed. So what did
he do? He crawled out of bed, wrapped himself in a sheet (I
have no idea what had happened to his clothes), and arrived
in the Garden of Gethsemane. There he stood, trying to look
like an olive tree. And then the people came with Judas and
arrested Jesus. When everyone else scattered, he ran, too.
There was only one problem—someone reached out and
grabbed the sheet, so he had to run away naked. What a start
to young John Mark's attempt to follow Christ!

Well, John Mark grew up a bit and the apostle Paul came
along and said, "Now, I need two people to go along with me
on this missionary journey." And Barnabas said, "I'm your
man. And why don't we take young John Mark? He's a good
kid. He wants to be a missionary." "All right," said Paul,
"fine." So they went. And John Mark was their assistant, their
servant, their business manager. He got the boat tickets and
arranged for hospitality and became their secretary. Then
right in the middle of the toughest assignment that Paul and
Barnabas had ever had, John Mark got scared and ran home.

After a while the time came again for another missionary
journey and Barnabas said, "Let's give John Mark another

chance." What a picture of love that covers! Barnabas was always running around throwing a blanket of love over everybody's faults. Let's give him another chance, he said. Forget about the past; it's covered, just as Christ covered our failings. Paul didn't agree, and the Bible says the contention was so strong between Paul and Barnabas that they split up. They don't appear as a team again. Barnabas took the side of John Mark, and there's no doubt in my mind that at that point he was right and Paul was wrong. In fact, we know he was. For later in life Paul sends for John Mark and says, "He's profitable to me." If Barnabas hadn't seen something redeemable in that utter failure of a young man, we wouldn't have our Gospel of Mark. As a matter of fact, Barnabas had seen the potential in Saul of Tarsus, too, when he was newly converted. It was Barnabas who accepted him when others feared and rejected him (Acts 9:26-27).

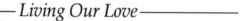

## *Living Our Love*

Who do you know who has "failed" in some way in his or her Christian walk? How can you love that person in a way that covers faults and failings and aids in healing and restoration?

# Love perseveres

> Let us fix our eyes on Jesus, the author and
> perfecter of our faith, who for the joy set before him
> endured the cross, scorning its shame, and sat down
> at the right hand of the throne of God. Consider
> him who endured such opposition from sinful men,
> so that you will not grow weary and lose heart.
>
> —*Hebrews 12:2*

Love not only bears all things, believes all things, hopes all things, but it endures all things, too (KJV). Love is able to abide with a restful attitude under whatever comes along.

Maybe you're disappointed and you've hoped and you've hoped for things to be better, but now you've come to the end of your life and you're still disappointed. Nothing has turned out the way you wanted; you're discouraged and ready to quit. Don't quit—remember that love endures all things. Love hangs in there no matter what.

During World War II there was a ship called the HMS Eskimo. It had been in a horrendous sea battle, taken a torpedo hit that had destroyed its bows and effectively cut the ship in half. Everybody thought that was the end of the Eskimo, but one day it sailed into Barrow Shipyard. As it steamed into port, the whole country seemed to be there cheering, crying, and waving. The men stood to attention on the shattered deck, saluted the flag that, though ripped to shreds, still waved bravely, and sang the national anthem. I will never forget seeing that ship—or what was left of it— battered but safely in port.

That's what endurance means. It means you might even have to arrive home in heaven like the HMS Eskimo. But you'll go home standing tall and straight. You'll go home still believing. You'll go home still enduring what must be endured. You'll go home still trusting God—even though you've been torpedoed right in half!

If you look at church history, you'll see many, many believers in Jesus who endured the unimaginable. But you'll read the stories and find that they were victorious in death, and they were at peace. How? Because they knew where they were going and who they belonged to, and they were able to endure the worst. They recognized this life as so insignificant when compared to eternity with God and his Son. There are times when that larger view of things is what we must have to get through the present. God's love of us makes our love able to endure.

## Living Our Love

Read a biography of a Christian—missionary, saint, ministry leader, whatever—and take note of the kinds of trials that person has had to endure. Allow the testimony of other Christians to encourage your own endurance.

# "Love never fails"

> Love never fails. But where there are prophecies, they will cease; where there are tongues, they will be stilled; where there is knowledge, it will pass away. For we know in part and we prophesy in part, but when perfection comes, the imperfect disappears.
>
> —*1 Corinthians 13:8*

The final description of love in this "love chapter" is that love is eternally relevant.

Saying that "love never fails" doesn't mean that loving is a simplistic answer to anything, that love always works. If a girl determines to love a man to death, there is no guarantee that he will love her. If he doesn't respond, nothing can be done. "Love never fails" doesn't mean that love will always achieve whatever you want. It doesn't mean that love never fails to get a response, but rather that love never fails to love!

Love never gives up. Love always abides. Love is of eternal significance. Love never quits!

Shakespeare wrote:

> Love is not love
> which alters when it alteration finds,
> or bends with the remover to remove:
> Oh, no! It is an ever-fixed mark,
> that looks on tempests and is never shaken;
> It is the star to every wandering bark,
> whose worth's unknown, although his height
>    be taken.
>
> —*Sonnet 116*

"Love never fails" says to us that love will ultimately win over lack of love, just as God's love through Jesus' death and resurrection triumphed over death and hatred. In other words, whatever we do out of love will count. We may not see it counting at this moment—as this person doesn't respond or that bad thing happens anyway—but because love is the essence of God, any loving we do has an eternal place and purpose. As God looks over the span of our lives, he will see all the loving we did; it will certainly count. Love may be ignored, but it is never wasted, and—in God's book— never discounted.

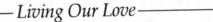

## *Living Our Love*

Think of a situation you are tempted to give up on because of a lack of response to your love. Tell God that if you fail to get a response you will never fail to go on loving.

# "Faith, hope and love"

And now these three remain: faith, hope and love.
But the greatest of these is love. —*1 Corinthians 13:13*

Something that becomes evident without much meditation is that these three qualities—faith, hope, and love—go together. You can't pick and choose among them. The Bible draws a picture of these three graces as inextricably related and bound up in each other.

Faith is at the root of human experience. When you have *faith* in a valid object of faith, it produces hope. *Hope* becomes a branch that grows out of the root of faith. When you become a person of faith and hope, you develop a faith and hope in other people and in God, and that leads you to love God and love people. *Love* is the ultimate fruit.

Of these three superb Christian graces—absolutely interrelated, absolutely indispensable—love is still the greatest. We don't need to diminish faith or diminish hope in order to glorify love. Instead, we need to upgrade both faith and hope; and that allows love to flourish. Without hope, we become pessimistic and lethargic. Why do anything, since everything is such a mess anyway? That certainly isn't conducive to love. And faith is the ability to see what God sees—the divine potential he's planted in people. Faith keeps us from giving up on one another. Faith sees ahead, and love energizes growth toward that vision. Without faith, we could only be sentimental and *wish* that things might work out, cry over another person's struggles, without the confidence that the struggles won't have the last word.

And what do we have if love is missing? Love is our ability to act in such a way that we build up others and ourselves. Love is action that springs from the very goodness and holiness of God. Love is what makes it all happen. That's why it's the greatest of the three. Love is actually God's very character translated into something tangible for us to know.

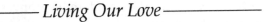
## Living Our Love

Think of a person who has loved you consistently for most of your life. What did *love* cause that person to do? How has love been manifested in that person's words and actions toward you? And how has God's love manifested itself in *your* life? Where is love missing in your life? What can you do about those "gaps"?

# Love without pretense

> Listen, my dear brothers: Has not God chosen those
> who are poor in the eyes of the world to be rich in
> faith and to inherit the kingdom he promised those
> who love him? But you have insulted the poor.
>
> —James 2:5-6

We leave 1 Corinthians for a while to benefit from the very practical teachings about love in the letter of James. In this passage, this early church leader rebukes the believers because they have insulted the people God has chosen and enriched. Can you imagine anything worse for those who hold to the faith in the Lord Jesus Christ than to insult those whom God has honored? That's what James is saying the believers have done. With interesting irony, James goes on to point out that the very people the believers are fawning over with preferential treatment are actually the ones who are giving them a hard time.

James says a few verses ahead of this passage that "as believers in our glorious Lord Jesus Christ, don't show favoritism." I think it's significant that James uses Jesus' full title: Lord Jesus Christ. *Lord* reminds us that he is Lord of all. *Jesus* reminds us that he is the Savior who came and died for all. *Christ* reminds us that he is the Messiah, the Sent One, who came from heaven's glory for all people. Those who want to "hold the faith" of God must have an all-encompassing view of who he is. If he is the Lord of all, then how can I discriminate against someone who falls under his lordship? If Jesus died for all, then how can I have less of an opinion of a person than Jesus had when he died for him? And if God sent his Christ into the world with all people in mind, how can I possibly decide that some people are less significant than others when

God has said, in sending his Son, that all people are fundamentally the same?

The illustration James gives here shows us prejudice and preferential treatment, but it illustrates pretense as well. Notice James 2:4: "Have you not discriminated among yourselves and become judges with evil thoughts?" The word translated "discriminated" is used elsewhere in the book of James as "wavered" or "doubted" (1:6). And the phrase translated "among yourselves" could equally be translated "within yourself." Some commentators believe that it also means "you are wavering and doubting within your individual hearts." Think of it that way for a moment. James seems to be asking us, "If you find yourself majoring on your likes and avoiding your dislikes, at the same time claiming to hold the faith of the Lord Jesus Christ, aren't you really wavering inside your heart? Aren't you a living contradiction?"

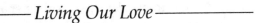

## Living Our Love

In what ways do your actions and attitudes contradict your Christian beliefs? How can you adjust your lifestyle to better reflect your life of faith and love?

# Love doesn't discriminate

> "Love the Lord your God with all your heart and
> with all your soul and with all your mind." This is
> the first and greatest commandment. And the
> second is like it: "Love your neighbor as yourself."
> All the Law and the Prophets hang on these two
> commandments.
> —*Matthew 22:37-40*

I (Stuart) was born in England in 1930. World War II started
in 1939, so during my adolescence, our family had bombs
whistling around our ears. The bombs came from Germany;
we could see the planes bringing them over. We heard the
propaganda. We heard the messages of Mr. Churchill. We did
not like Germans. And that was understandable, since they
seemed to be intent on bombing us to extinction.

Then several Germans were taken prisoner and were quar-
tered in a prison close to where we lived. The authorities got
in touch with the boys in our neighborhood, including myself,
and asked us to put together a soccer team to play the prisoners of war. It was a great idea except that we were so much
younger than they were. So we youngsters said, "Sure, we'll
take on those Jerrys!" We laid our plans for kicking their
ankles and shins to get even with them for all the bombs they
dropped on us.

But something strange happened. Once we started playing
soccer with those prisoners of war, we lost interest in bombs
and Jerrys and who belonged to which group. We discovered
that they were pretty good—and we were pretty good. We
had fun! They hurt and they laughed and they shouted and
they kicked and they were just like us. Our problem was that
we'd been working on the basis of prejudice—or pre-judging.
We had assumed that all Germans were the same—crooks—

and we wanted nothing to do with them. As we got to know what they were really like, we discovered how wrong we had been.

So we were enlightened about the Germans, but we still made fun of the Italians. To us, it seemed that the Italians had their war machine perpetually in reverse; they were always making strategic withdrawals. They advanced backwards. We had no time for them. Then our community received some Italian prisoners of war, and the invitation came again to play soccer with them. What happened? We discovered that Guiseppe was a pretty nice fellow and that Leonardo was a great right-winger. We found that we actually had been prisoners of our own prejudices. We found that our likes and dislikes were not founded on reality at all.

What were the actions of the Lord Jesus Christ toward those who were being discriminated against? One day he went through Samaria and sat down with a woman and immediately burst through two cultural taboos: first, men didn't talk to women; and second, Jews didn't talk to Samaritans. Jesus came as God's Anointed One to all people. He's our example. So one thing comes through loud and clear: Attitudes and actions that are discriminatory are utterly and totally out of order for believers. Love never discriminates.

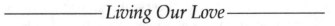

## Living Our Love

What groups of people are often discriminated against in society in general? In your community? At your workplace? In your church? Take specific steps to include those who are often alienated.

# Prejudice in church

> Suppose a man comes into your meeting wearing a
> gold ring and fine clothes, and a poor man also
> comes in. If you show special attention to the man
> wearing fine clothes and say, "Here's a good seat for
> you," but say to the poor man, "You stand there" or
> "Sit on the floor, by my feet," have you not
> discriminated among yourselves and become
> judges with evil thoughts?                    —James 2:2-4

Have you ever done that? James saw it happening in the
church of God. He gives a perfect example of prejudice and
of preferential treatment. A good seat for the rich man! Have
you ever heard someone say in regard to someone else,
"Wouldn't he make a wonderful Christian?" or "Wouldn't she
make a wonderful Christian?" We're thinking, *That's a person
who's got what it takes,* or *She's really loaded with money,* or *He
really knows what he's doing,* or *She's got prestige,* or *He has
position.* We're thinking that if such a person came to Christ,
he'd bring all his wealth and prestige to the church—to
us—along with him. We'd be as prestigious as he is. He could
make things happen for us. So Christians go ahead and target
such a person, giving him the best seat and special treatment.
That's preferential treatment, operating only on the basis of
external, material considerations. It overlooks the fact that we
claim to be holding to the faith of the Lord Jesus Christ, his
gospel of love that hooks on the inside of a person—not the
outside.

Imagine the situation that may have prompted James's
words above. You've got a small group of believers, and James
is the leader of this little church. It's made up mostly of poor
people—some of them slaves—and very few wealthy or

influential people at all. One day, to their delight, someone very wealthy, very influential, and very powerful comes in. Of course, the people say, "Wow! That's great! Double the offering overnight." They become very deferential to him, fawning over him and looking after him, ushering him to the best seat. But they discover a shabby little man in the seat, so they try to get him out of there because they don't want the influential man to see the shabby little man lest he won't come back.

What's going on is a perfect example of prejudice. The believers are pre-judging both men on purely external and material criteria. They are not showing any interest in the internal realities of the people or in the spiritual realities of the people, and they don't seem to have any idea that the Lord is the Lord of both, that Jesus is the Savior of both, and that Christ came for both. They have committed prejudice in the church of Jesus Christ.

When we run into problems, it's easy to get sidetracked from the problem by a person. Then instead of addressing the problem, we attack the person. This had probably happened among the believers to whom James was writing. They had perhaps failed to address the problems, they had found the person they identified with the problem, they had attacked that person, and then they had decided that a whole lot of people who belonged to his group were all the same. That's how prejudice often works. Love and prejudice never go together.

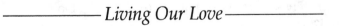

*Living Our Love*

What type of person might feel uncomfortable in your church, and why? What can you do toward eliminating such prejudice in love?

# Love welcomes those who "don't fit"

> [The expert in the law] answered, " . . . Love your
> neighbor as yourself." "You have answered
> correctly," Jesus replied. "Do this and you will live."
> But he wanted to justify himself, so he asked Jesus,
> "And who is my neighbor?" —*Luke 10:27-29*

Shortly after I (Stuart) began my ministry at Elmbrook
Church, there was a certain gentleman who came to me with
a complaint.

"About these young people you've brought into church,"
he began.

I was confused. "What young people?"

"All these hippies. People with blue jeans with holes
patched with the American flag. Sweatshirts and bootlaces
tied round their necks. Long hair. Flowers behind their ears.
You've brought all these people in here!"

"I didn't bring them in," I answered. "I just happen to
believe that because some of our people were reaching them
and they weren't being welcomed into our church before now,
it was about time we welcomed them. But because there are
only five hundred of us, I understand that a hundred of them
suddenly showing up on our doorstep can cause quite a stir.
Especially when they arrive in brightly painted buses!"

"Well, about these young people," he continued fiercely,
"you've got to understand one thing. They have got to be kept
completely separate from our young people. Do you understand?"

"I understand," I said.

"Really?" He seemed surprised. "I thought I was going to
have such a battle with you. You really understand that?"

"I understand, of course. There's absolutely nothing new about that approach. They've had it in South Africa for years; it's called apartheid. It's a system based on prejudice and fear. If you want to operate the church of Christ on the basis of prejudice and fear, go right ahead. But count me out because we've got something that transcends prejudice and transcends fear and will not allow us to do that kind of separating. They are as welcome here as you."

It was an interesting Saturday morning. But I'll give credit to that man. Although he came in with that attitude, as we studied the Word of God and prayed together, he totally reversed his position. He left with the comment, "Okay, let's get to it. Let's integrate these young people into our church."

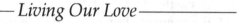

## *Living Our Love*

Make plans to welcome someone into your "circle"—at work, church, or in the neighborhood—who would not automatically fit.

# Love makes unlikely friends

> The LORD does not look at the things man looks at.
> Man looks at the outward appearance, but the LORD
> looks at the heart.                    —*1 Samuel 16:7*

There are times when I (Stuart) have evaluated people according to externals. The day I joined the Marines I saw a fellow with the meanest, ugliest face I'd ever seen. I determined to stay out of his way no matter what. An army captain had told me when I entered the Marines, "Make sure they know you're a Christian the first night you're there. Kneel by your bed and pray—that'll tell them right away." I was less than enthusiastic about that. "They'll probably throw boots at you," the army captain said. "If they do, clean them and return them."

So with this good advice, I embarked on my career in the Royal Marines. I waited until all the men in my barracks room were all busy in the other end of the room, then slipped down beside my bed, trying to look as though I had lost something under the bed. I knew they'd seen me because a loud silence descended upon the room, except for the creaking of floorboards that told me they were walking toward me. I could feel them gather around the bed. Immediately the only thing I was praying was "Help!" A legitimate prayer. I counted in my head up to twenty-five and then got up. "Have you lost something?" one of them asked. "He was praying," pitched in another. "Who to?" said another. "God!" "Is he under the bed?" They had never really seen anybody pray; the idea was foreign to them. They weren't particularly hostile. But they were amused, and I felt awfully stupid.

And then the really ugly, mean-looking one said, "Consider the lilies. They toil not. Neither do they spin. But I say unto you that Solomon, in all his glory, is not arrayed like unto one of these." Everybody looked at him. "Who's Solomon?" asked one marine. "What's this 'arrayed with glory' stuff?" asked another. "Who wants lilies?"

The big, ugly man said, "It's the Bible. I was quoting from the Bible to you." I discovered that the mean, ugly man—the one who looked like such a cutthroat—could recite Scripture by the yard! I discovered that he was one of the most courageous people I have ever known. We became inextricably bound up in each other's lives. I saved his life, and he saved mine, more than once. We became inseparable. I did eventually find out the reason for his incredible face; he was the middle-weight boxing champion of England. He didn't tell me himself; he didn't need to brag about his accomplishments. That was the kind of person he was. He was one of the greatest people I ever met, and I had initially written him off after one look. I couldn't have been more wrong!

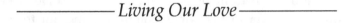

## Living Our Love

Make an effort to get to know someone you wouldn't naturally be attracted to.

# Love isn't a crowd pleaser

Haughty eyes and a proud heart, the lamp of the
wicked, are sin!                                  —*Proverbs 21:4*

Have you ever met a crowd pleaser at a party? Love doesn't
need to act like that because love is content with itself. Love
is at peace. Love is satisfied with being the person that you
really are, not making a show of the person you're not. So love
doesn't perform. Jesus was tempted in this way. "Throw
yourself down from the pinnacle of the temple," the devil
said. In other words, "Put on a big show—a big act." Jesus
rejected that particular approach because love makes no parade.

Remember the crocodile passage from Job? It reads, "He
[the crocodile] leaves a shining furrow in his wake." He
specializes in great entrances and dramatic exits. That's pride.
Love makes no parade. I've seen somebody make an entrance
to a stage once in front of thousands of people. We were
meeting for prayer in the wings before walking out to the
stage together to take our seats. But this particular person
wouldn't. She would meet and pray with us but she wouldn't
walk out and sit down with us because she wanted to make
an entrance. And believe it or not, she stayed in the wings until
it was time for her to speak and then she came on stage. All I
could think about was "love makes no parade. Love doesn't
swagger. Love isn't showy."

You know what love does? Love tiptoes in and serves and
leaves unnoticed. It's what Jesus did. He tiptoed into a woman's
womb. Did he make a shining entrance? He certainly could
have if he'd wanted to. But love makes no parade. Love

doesn't vaunt itself, is not puffed up. Love doesn't perform. Love can take publicity or leave it.

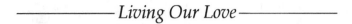

## *Living Our Love*

Spend some time reflecting on your habits when you're around people. What do you do to get attention? How do you put on airs? Are you guilty of false modesty? How do you respond to attention? Pray for wisdom in the way you relate to others—a way that gives honor to yourself as God's child and creation, but does not go after praise of the crowd.

# Love is something you do

As the body without the spirit is dead, so faith
without deeds is dead.                                    —*James 2:26*

$F$ortunately we don't just have the overall dimensions of what love is. Scripture gives us careful, meticulous descriptions of many aspects of love. It's important to take a close look at the sixteen descriptions of love in 1 Corinthians 13:4-7 and not get sidetracked when reading it simply because it is so familiar or because it is so beautiful. There are rugged, abrasive realities in this passage that describe what love really is when it is in operation.

Love is something that you do, and something that you don't do. This can be a surprise to some people because it's easy to fall into the trap of thinking that love is basically something that you *feel*. Love is not primarily something that you feel. The more I look at Scripture, the more convinced I am that love is something that you do and something that you don't do, whether you feel like it or not. Feeling like it just makes things easier.

Think about these characteristics: Patience doesn't lose its temper or get pushy; kindness makes the right response rather than the natural one; love does not boast; love does not promote oneself (pride); love holds its tongue and respects others rather than acting rudely; love learns how not to be provoked by temper; love makes a point to forget the wrongs people have committed; love doesn't join the applause when the bad guy "gets his"; love applauds when good things happen even to undeserving people; love goes through the day believing and acting as if God and people are trustworthy; love makes the effort to cover over the sins of others so that they may be healed and restored, rather than publicly humiliated and flogged; love keeps going no matter what the circumstances.

You see, love *is* something you do or refrain from doing. You cannot love with God's love, merely by *ooohing* and *aaahing* over the "love chapter." The Scriptures require action.

## —————— *Living Our Love* ——————

As we have seen, the "love chapter" is a portrait of the Lord Jesus. But it is also a challenging portrait of the believer. After the description we are exhorted to "follow the way of love" (1 Corinthians 14:1). Is that realistic? Yes and no. No: We cannot do it perfectly because we are fallen, failing people. But yes: We can grow in these aspects of love because the Christ who fulfilled them in his own life lives in us. By his Spirit, he reproduces his loving living through us as we trust him to do what he has promised to do, and obey him by doing what he has told us to do.

# Prayer

Dear Father;
Whose very nature is to care,
see us here,
Your own forever family,
Suspended in time and space,
turning our thoughts toward Thee.

Dear God,
Whose very nature is to love,
So fan the flames of all our relationships,
that they may be a warm place
where children love to play,
where people live to give each other
room to breathe and space to grow.

Dear Lord,
Whose very nature is to give,
Teach us what that means,
That Jesus, Savior of our lives
may lend his power
of giving
to our selfish hearts.

And oh, dear Teacher,
so show us how to model Christ in all his
sweet simplicity and strength . . .
that seeing him in me, others shall inherit
Gold faith!—
Trust, tried in the crucible of life,
my gift to them—
a godly heritage.

Amen.

Adapted from "Gold Faith" by Jill Briscoe in *Heartbeat* (Shaw Publishers, 1991)

PART 3

# The Impact of Love

The cure for all the ills and wrongs, the cares, the sorrows, and the crimes of humanity, all lie in that one word *love*. It is the divine vitality that everywhere produces and restores life. To each and every one of us, it gives the power of working miracles if we will.

—*Lydia Maria Child*

# Awestruck by God's love

O LORD, our Lord,
how majestic is your name in all the earth!
... When I consider your heavens,
the work of your fingers,
the moon and the stars,
which you have set in place,
what is man that you are mindful of him,
the son of man that you care for him?

—*Psalm 8:1, 3-4*

If you go on a vacation to the mountains, you might get up early and discover an astounding sunrise, backdropped by beautiful scenery, and all of nature singing. You find yourself joining in a hymn of praise deep in your heart. You are awestruck with God's tremendous creative power. Have you ever had that experience?

If we are awestruck by the power of God that is manifested in creation, then we should be equally awestruck with the love of God toward us, manifested in Jesus Christ. His love, power, holiness, grace, and mercy are all equivalent to his own nature. His creative power is so beyond our ability to make something that it is mind-boggling. His love for us is so beyond our capacity for love that it should utterly astound us.

On the sidelines of the stoning of Stephen (Acts 7:54-60) stood a man called Saul of Tarsus, literally presiding over the martyrdom of Stephen. This is our introduction to a person who is going to be a crucial figure throughout the rest of the Scriptures and in church history. Saul had an experience that changed him from being the arch-enemy of Christ into being the great apostle of the Christian gospel. Saul (later called "Paul") describes what happened himself, saying that he finally discovered that Christ, the Son of God, loved him and gave himself for him. Paul never recovered from that discovery.

Basically, that's the essence of spiritual existence: to discover that the Son of God loves you personally and gave himself for you and to allow yourself to be enraptured by that discovery—motivated by it to live the rest of your life in the good of it. As we understand the love of God toward us, the love from us to God is stimulated. And as we begin to express our love to God, we begin to see people in a new light; we see them as objects of God's love. As the love of God enraptures us, stimulates us to love him, changes our attitudes toward people, we begin to be motivated to share the love of God to those who have not yet discovered God's love, and thus can't live in the good of it. This is how loving God and loving people become so intertwined.

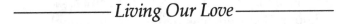 *Living Our Love*

Recall a time when God's love has astounded you. How did that incident change your life?

# Compelled by God's love

> For Christ's love compels us, because we are
> convinced that one died for all, and therefore all
> died. And he died for all, that those who live should
> no longer live for themselves but for him who died
> for them and was raised again. So from now on we
> regard no one from a worldly point of view. Though
> we once regarded Christ in this way, we do so no
> longer. Therefore, if anyone is in Christ, he is a new
> creation; the old has gone, the new has come! All
> this is from God, who reconciled us to himself
> through Christ and gave us the ministry of
> reconciliation: that God was reconciling the world
> to himself in Christ, not counting men's sins against
> them. And he has committed to us the message of
> reconciliation. We are therefore Christ's ambassadors,
> as though God were making his appeal through us.
> We implore you on Christ's behalf: Be reconciled to
> God. God made him who had no sin to be sin for us,
> so that in him we might become the righteousness of
> God.                                    —*2 Corinthians 5:14-21*

Notice that Paul starts off with "For Christ's love compels
us." The word literally means "hems us in"; we can't get away
from it. Whichever way we turn, we're confronted with the
message of the love of Christ. Sometimes we view religion as
something "nice." It has its place. But the nice place that it has
is rather peripheral to our lives instead of central. We want it
to be a sort of additive. All the other good things we do in life
should include—along with them—religion. We don't want
religion to become too intense or dominant. We're nervous

about letting religion become the focal point of our experience and the motivation of our lives.

If that is our attitude toward religion, the Scriptures have some straightforward words for us. They say that if we believe that God loved us in Christ so much that he gave Christ to die for us, that Christ was not spared and that he did not spare himself, then the only logical and appropriate response to that is, "I will no longer live for myself, but for him, because he didn't live for himself, but for me."

If I *say* that I believe God loved me when I was a sinner and Christ died for me in my hopeless condition, and yet that stays peripheral, an additive, to my life, then I clearly have not grasped this belief. Because if I believe that Christ died for me, how can I keep him peripheral? If he was raised to be Lord, how can I relegate him to the position of additive? If the gospel is true, if the love of God is real, if the death of Christ is efficacious, it means that understanding what it means will cause me to choose to live for him. As an old hymn proclaims, "Love so amazing, so divine, demands my life, my love, my all."

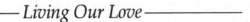

## *Living Our Love*

Evaluate the role that "religion" plays in your life right now. Is it just one compartment? How can you better integrate what you believe into what you do from day to day?

# Passionate about God's love

> O God, you are my God,
> earnestly I seek you;
> my soul thirsts for you,
> my body longs for you,
> in a dry and weary land
> where there is no water.
>
> —*Psalm 63:1*

We begin to say with the apostle Paul, "When I was a sinner—powerless, ungodly, an enemy—you, of your own volition and because of your nature, reached out and loved me to such an extent, you sent Christ to die for me. That is mind-boggling." Ask yourself an honest question. Do you have a cool, calculating approach to religion? Or a burning intensity fueled by your understanding of the love of God?

Considering God's love in terms of theology is a beginning place, but let's get it into our bloodstream—into the realm of personal emotion and experience. This is what happened to Saul of Tarsus. After the execution of Stephen, great persecution arose against the followers of the Way in Jerusalem. Saul was behind it all. Then he decided to go to Damascus and hunt out some followers of the Way and exterminate them there as well. But he hadn't reckoned on divine intervention. On the way he had a vision of some kind. The net result was that his life was turned around 180 degrees. He went to Damascus to destroy the followers of the Way; he ended up in Damascus, preaching Christ and being run out of town himself.

That's what you call a conversion! The question is, what in the world happened to him? Saul says he had a vision of Christ. This vision threw light on two things: on Christ, and on Saul. In burning intensity, Saul saw who Christ really is and what Christ had really done. And Saul saw himself for what he was—zealous, but terribly misled and actually on the wrong side of the battle. Up until this point, he had seen neither of these things. But from that point, the vision meant tangible changes in his life.

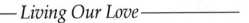

## Living Our Love

Review the ways in which you have viewed Jesus Christ in your life, beginning with childhood. How has your picture and understanding of Jesus changed as you grew up and grew in your faith? What kinds of changes have occurred in your life because of the new understandings you've had about who Jesus is?

# God's love is practical

Teach me, O LORD, to follow your decrees;
then I will keep them to the end.
Give me understanding and I will keep your law
and obey it with all my heart.
Direct me in the path of your commands,
for there I find delight.
Turn my heart toward your statutes
and not toward selfish gain.

—*Psalm 119:33-36*

Love not only has divine qualities, but it is completely practical. Love is putting into practice the concern for others' well-being over my own well-being. We've already explored how the whole of 1 Corinthians 13 is instruction in practical love.

Ministers and preachers need to be reminded of love's practicality probably more than any other group of people. Why? Because we deal with faith and religion on a theological level, and it's very easy to get stuck there, without ever making the sermon or lesson applicable to those who hear.

For example, at the end of a sermon I've preached, I could say to myself, "That was masterly; that was perfectly clear." But then someone walks up to me and tells me, "I didn't understand a word you said. That was way over my head." My natural response to that is: "Elevate your head!" A lady once told me, "My preacher preaches right over our heads. What should we do?" I told her, "Stand on tip-toe!"

Obviously, I'm particularly impatient with these people because they do not seem to understand that they have the unbelievable privilege of sitting under my remarkable, superb teaching! That's my problem—with a ready solution of being primarily concerned with their well-being instead of my own. My sermon may have been crystal clear to me, but to the person who didn't understand, it was not. Because God commands me to be concerned about that person's well-being, it's got to be more important to me to help him understand than to be receiving praise for what I thought was a masterly sermon.

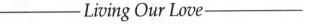
## Living Our Love

In what area(s) of life are you tempted to keep your religion at a theological or philosophical level, and not make it practical? What steps can you take toward faith/love in practice?

# Taking steps toward the goal

> The goal of this command is love, which comes from a pure heart and a good conscience and a sincere faith. Some have wandered away from these and turned to meaningless talk.    —*1 Timothy 1:5-6*

We set goals in our business life, in physical fitness, and in the way we run our homes. In fact, we set goals in any undertaking that is important to us.

So what about goals in loving? Here are three practical ways to get started.

**1. Evaluation.** Have you honestly established love as a goal in each relationship? As a parent, are you more concerned with how you'll look when your children are grown instead of their well-being? Or as a wife, are you more preoccupied with your husband meeting your expectations than with your loving him?

Do you get upset with someone because they disagree with you over a minute point, or can you honestly say that though you disagree, you are still concerned primarily with their well-being?

If you find upon evaluation that you are sadly lacking in the area of pursuing love as a goal, you're in good company. I expect that 99.9 percent of us will discover the same thing. That pushes us to step two.

**2. Reconciliation.** Reconciliation means you take steps to deal with what is wrong. Until you evaluate relationships, you may never realize that things are wrong between yourself and another person. Once you do, you must move toward reconciliation. And *you're* the one who takes the first step. At this point you can't afford to say, "Well, if he wants to get things right with me, he can come to me. I didn't do anything. He offended *me*." You can't assume that he is reading this book—but you are! You are the one to whom God is speaking, to whom the Spirit of God is revealing truth.

Remember, though, that when you take specific steps toward rectifying what's wrong you must anticipate being misunderstood. The person you've offended may have been watching for some sign of weakness in you that he can capitalize on. The minute you come toward him in steps of reconciliation, he may recognize the moment he's been waiting for. So as you stretch out your hand, you may get your finger bitten. But keep reaching out anyway.

**3. Consolidation.** Loving relationships require work; they don't just happen. Love is something you do whether you feel like it or not. A relationship that is going to succeed in love takes work or it will disintegrate instead of consolidate. Without consolidation you will never break free from an unending pattern of evaluation and reconciliation because every time you evaluate you will find something else to rectify between you. What's needed is that ongoing attitude—the attitude that consolidates the relationship. As you succeed in this area, God will send more people along for you to love. So Christians who are doing what God has commanded, in the power of the Holy Spirit, never need to feel bored! There is always someone to love.

———————— *Living Our Love* ————————

Using the above steps, map out some love goals for this week and month.

# Loving God

> "Father, the time has come. Glorify your Son, that
> your Son may glorify you. For you granted him
> authority over all people that he might give eternal
> life to all those you have given him. Now this is
> eternal life: that they may know you, the only true
> God, and Jesus Christ, whom you have sent."
>
> —*John 17:1-3*

The Bible speaks of our loving God. We run into all kinds of
problems at this level. If our concept of love at this point is
basically emotional—only sentimental feelings—we will
never grapple with what it means to love God. How can we
feel sentimental about God? How can we get romantic with
him? Christian music might enhance a sentimental mood, but
how long can those feelings be maintained? We can't be
surrounded by sentimental music twenty-four hours a day.
Even if you play it nonstop to keep the mood mellow, there
are limits.

To love God truly is not to have sentimental, romantic, and,
of course, not sexual feelings about God. The Bible tells us
from the beginning what is involved with loving God: You
shall love God with all your heart and with all your soul and
with all your strength.

The heart is the part of you that discerns, so to love God is
first of all to discern the truth about him. It's an intelligent
thing, a grasping of truth about God. *You love God not because
of feelings but because of truth.* But the truth is not a dry,
desiccated truth. It's a truth that involves your soul, the part
of you that desires. So having *discerned* the truth of God, you
*desire* to know more of him and respond to what he is. And

it's not just desire because you love him with your *strength*—
the part of you that decides and acts on a decision.

So what does it mean to love God? It means to have an
all-around relationship where, discerning him and desiring
him, you decide to put him first with all your strength.

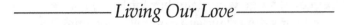 *Living Our Love*

Have you tried to love God primarily through emotions? What have been the limitations of that method?
How can you love God with your heart and soul and
strength?

# Loving my neighbor

> Do not defraud your neighbor or rob him. Do not
> hold back the wages of a hired man overnight. Do
> not curse the deaf or put a stumbling block in front
> of the blind, but fear your God. . . . Do not pervert
> justice . . . judge your neighbor fairly. Do not go
> about spreading slander among your people. Do
> not do anything that endangers your neighbor's
> life. . . . Do not hate your brother in your heart.
> Rebuke your neighbor frankly so you will not share
> in his guilt. Do not seek revenge or bear a grudge
> against one of your people, but love your neighbor
> as yourself. I am the LORD.            —*Leviticus 19:13-18*

The corollary to loving God is to love my neighbor as myself. We ask, "Who is my neighbor? The guy next door, or the woman cater-corner from my house? The family down the street?"

Somebody once asked the same question in the hearing of the Lord Jesus. So Jesus sat the man down and told a story: "A certain man went down from Jerusalem to Jericho and fell among thieves." It was the tale about the Good Samaritan, and at the end of it the man knew the answer to the question, "Who is my neighbor?" *My neighbor is the person who within the sphere of my influence needs me.* Jesus provided a generalized definition of that neighbor and then pointed directly: your neighbor is the man in the ditch. As the man lay in the ditch, three people came by. The first said, "Sorry, I'm terribly busy," and went on his way. The second stood over the limp body and said, "You know, something really ought to be done. This is a disgrace!" and then went on his way. The Good Samaritan went down into the ditch himself to discover not only "Who is my neighbor?" but took time to know who his neighbor was. He bound up his wounds. He poured out oil and wine. He provided his donkey. He took the man to an inn.

Have you noticed how many people keep shut up tight in their own houses and yards? They want their privacy—they don't want neighbors to see them too closely. The flip side of that is that *they don't want to see their neighbors too closely, either.* After all, if we look too closely, we'll see the needs: the man who batters his wife inside their $200,000 home in the suburbs; the children alienated from parents; the person suffering in silence from depression, despair, and loneliness. It's much easier not to see any of that; then we won't be aware of how we should be loving our neighbors. But love doesn't hide its eyes and hurry by.

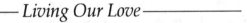

## *Living Our Love*

Who, within the sphere of your influence, needs your help and love? Ask God to guide you as you make a list of current "neighbors."

# Loving myself

> You created my inmost being; you knit me together
> in my mother's womb. I praise you because I am
> fearfully and wonderfully made; your works are
> wonderful, I know that full well. My frame was not
> hidden from you when I was made in the secret
> place. When I was woven together in the depths of
> the earth, your eyes saw my unformed body. All the
> days ordained for me were written in your book
> before one of them came to be.        —*Psalm 139:13-16*

I'm to love God and love my neighbor as I love myself. Yes—love myself. We are not instructed to love ourselves; it is assumed that we do. But some Christians tend to get confused. Jesus said we were to "deny ourselves" and he assumed we would love ourselves. We must differentiate between *selfishness* and a healthy view of personhood or selfhood. Selfishness is unacceptable. But a healthy view of self says this: "I was created by God for a purpose. I was redeemed by God through the precious blood of Christ. I am indwelt by God's Spirit. I have been called and commissioned to a ministry. I have eternal significance. I cannot downgrade myself. I recognize that if I am to be what I was created and redeemed and ordained and called and anointed and ind-welled and equipped to be, then I'll take myself seriously and love myself properly. This is not selfishness but rather seeing myself as what I am through the grace of God. It's agreeing with God.

We find it easier to love ourselves when we know that others value us, don't we? To be appreciated and loved—that inspires us to care about ourselves. We must remember these basic facts: God died for us. Christ lives for us. And the Holy

Spirit dwells inside us. We should be honored to have God himself resident in us. And he doesn't merely live in the larger, corporate "us"; remember that Jesus spoke with *one* man named Nicodemus, *one* Samaritan woman at the well, *one* repentant thief on the nearby cross. *Each one of us* captures the attention, the interest, and the infinite love of God. How can we dare despise ourselves when the God of the universe has chosen us?

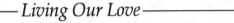

## Living Our Love

Think of all the things you've said to yourself lately that you would never say to another person, such as "How could you be so stupid!" "How could anyone be attracted to you?" "You'll probably never get anywhere; for every step forward, you jump five backward!" Ask God's forgiveness for the hateful way you have treated one for whom Christ died. Ask the Holy Spirit to "zap" you whenever you treat yourself in a way that is not loving.

# Loving my enemy

> Love your enemies and pray for those who persecute you, that you may be sons of your Father in heaven. He causes his sun to rise on the evil and the good, and sends rain on the righteous and the unrighteous.
> —*Matthew 5:44-45*

We're commanded to love God first. Next, we're to seek out the needy person within the sphere of our influence and get involved in that need. Then we're to recognize ourselves as who we are by the grace of God, take ourselves seriously, and love what God has made in us.

God also commands us to love our enemies. This means, minimally, that I will be prepared to reevaluate the conflict between that person and myself. And I'll be prepared to reconcile.

I'll need to remember, however, that I'm only responsible for my part and not for the other's response. Their reaction has to be left to the Lord.

When I (Jill) became a Christian, my very best friend became my enemy. It took me a long time to tell her I'd become a Christian because I knew she wouldn't like it. I was right. We shared a room in our college dorm, and the day I stumbled my way through a very elementary explanation of my faith my roommate slammed out of the room. That was the end of a great friendship. She never spoke to me again, and even though it hurt me greatly, I understood this was what "paying a price" meant. It was hard living with disapproval for the better part of a year.

I was certainly eager to reconcile, but I learned that it takes two. I did all I knew how to do and then had to just go on loving her, believing her reaction was her problem. She became my antagonist and yet the Lord helped me to go right on loving her.

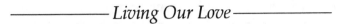

## *Living Our Love*

Are there any conflicts you need to evaluate? Any situations in which you need to attempt a reconciliation? Or maybe you have an antagonist for whom you can do nothing more. Talk over these situations with God in prayer, and ask the Holy Spirit to help you find ways to love those who do not want your love.

# Moved by Christ's love

Each one should use whatever gift he has received
to serve others, faithfully administering God's grace
in its various forms. If anyone speaks, he should do
it as one speaking the very words of God. If anyone
serves, he should do it with the strength God
provides, so that in all things God may be praised
through Jesus Christ. To him be the glory and the
power for ever and ever. Amen.          —*1 Peter 4:10-11*

Sometimes we need to learn through the more intuitive,
poetic parts of ourselves. Meditate on this.

Love listens—using silence to talk
louder than a thousand words—
bending near the sick one,
focusing attention
on the need.

Looking as though there's
no one else in the
wide, wide
world
Except the one who needs to talk.

Love is watertight, never leaking
the confidences shared at midnight—
or at dawn—or in the middle
of the day!
Time is irrelevant to love.

Love borrows wisdom from on high
passing on eternity's
information
at the right time and in
the right way.

Love's ears are open to a shriek
or groan, complaints or
angry shout.
It matters not—
No one listens
like Love!

Adapted from "Love Listens" by Jill Briscoe in *Heartbeat* (Shaw Publishers, 1991)

## *Living Our Love*

In what ways can you better love God and others?

# Love's joy—beyond circumstance

> I have learned to be content whatever the
> circumstances. I know what it is to be in need, and I
> know what it is to have plenty. I have learned the
> secret of being content in any and every situation,
> whether well fed or hungry, whether living in
> plenty or in want. I can do everything through him
> who gives me strength. —*Philippians 4:11-13*

Bill Fitch is a prominent Irish businessman. He is also an outspoken Christian. He and a number of other believers invited us to lead a series of meetings in Belfast. The hall where we were going to hold the meetings was bombed shortly before we got there, so we had to rent an alternative site. Hundreds and hundreds of young people came out for the first meeting, even though it was the first time the young people had been allowed in the inner city after curfew since "the troubles," as they call them, began.

On the final night of the meetings we got word that bombs had been planted in Bill's office block in the city center. We were having a meal together after the final meetings when the police called and told our friend that his building was on fire and asked him to come. So we went. The place was in flames; there was hardly anything left. Half the stairs had disappeared and most of the windows. The firemen were busy rescuing what they could, and we were allowed in through the smoke and flames and among the tangled hoses to see if anything could be salvaged.

It was quite frightening. I asked one of the firemen if he knew how many incendiary bombs had been planted and, if so, if they had all gone off. He said, "Well, I didn't count; I don't know." I kept asking, "Does anybody know? Are we even safe?" I felt very selfish, even though anyone would probably have felt the same way.

But in my anxiety over my own personal safety I'd forgotten Bill Fitch. He was standing in the middle of the ruins of his business—a scene of desolation. I was arrested by the man's face. He was totally composed and relaxed, and immediately I thought of the people who "took joyfully the spoiling of [their] goods" (Hebrews 10:34, KJV). A fireman came up to Bill in tears, saying, "Mr. Fitch, we know what you've tried to do for our city. We're going to work all night here to try and salvage some of these things for you." Bill just looked up and said, "No, you're not. I want you boys to go home. First of all, it's too dangerous here, and you're tired out anyway." And then he said, "Tomorrow is the Lord's day. We must be up bright and early to worship him."

I'll never forget that. Bill Fitch is a man who knows joy and contentment because he is confident in God's love for him, and it shows. His dependency is not on the abundance of the things that he possesses, but on a loving Lord. So, when they were taken from him, it didn't really matter. He still knew the love of God, and he loved God more than things.

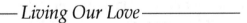 *Living Our Love*

What is your heart attached to in this life? Career? House? Keepsakes? Retirement accounts? Make a practice of turning these things over to God regularly, involving your heart primarily with him and his kingdom.

# For the love of diamonds

> These [trials] have come so that your faith—of
> greater worth than gold, which perishes even
> though refined by fire—may be proved genuine
> and may result in praise, glory and honor when
> Jesus Christ is revealed. Though you have not seen
> him, you love him; and even though you do not see
> him now, you believe in him and are filled with an
> inexpressible and glorious joy, for you are receiving
> the goal of your faith, the salvation of your souls.
>
> —*1 Peter 1:7-9*

Many years ago there were some children playing on a small hill in South Africa. One of them found a pretty pebble. The children began to throw it back and forth to each other. A man riding by on a horse noticed the children's excitement and stopped to question them. "What have you found?" he asked. "A pebble to play with," they answered. But the man knew they had found a diamond! He took the diamond to the city, and the most famous diamond rush in the world began. Thousands of people converged on that area of South Africa, looking for diamonds. The authorities determined how a claim could be staked and a day was set.

The would-be miners trained for two weeks, lifting and jogging. On the big day they lined up behind a line, a flag was dropped, and the diamond miners rushed! They put everything they had into getting out there and staking their claims. What they staked out they kept and mined. With very primitive implements, they dug the biggest manmade hole on the face of the earth in Kimberly, South Africa. Seeing the vast hole, hundreds of feet deep and one mile in circumference, that they had dug in the earth prompted my curiosity about their motivation. What motivated them? Greed! Lust for diamonds. They killed each other, lost their families, and even starved and suffered from disease and deprivation—all for diamonds! I stood there thinking, *Oh God, if that's what people can do with motivation, just think what mark we could leave on this earth with the motivation of agape love.*

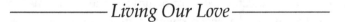

## Living Our Love

What are the forces that motivate you during a normal day?

# Love leads to hospitality

Share with God's people who are in need. Practice
hospitality.
—*Romans 12:13*

We may tend to think of Christian hospitality as a potluck
supper in the church basement or having the occasional missionary to dinner. In some cases, giving someone passing
through our city or someone in transition a place to stay may
come to mind. For many people, hospitality is coffee and pie
at my home after evening worship, or coffee and cookies at
someone else's home during the week. This can be a form of
hospitality, but it isn't what Paul meant by "practice hospitality." The word Paul uses is *philoxenia*, which literally means "the
love of strangers."

The apostle is teaching that believers should "be given to"
(KJV) the love of strangers. The expression "given to" is the
same idea as "setting our sights on," "hunting down," or
"establishing a goal." Imagine what it would be like if Christian believers would establish as a goal a specific concern for
strangers, and if they would set their sights on and lovingly
pursue it! One thing that would happen would be that no one
would ever leave our church fellowship saying, "That's an
unfriendly group." They might want to criticize us for bug-
ging them to death because we pursued them relentlessly in
love, but they could never accuse us of being disinterested.

In the early church hospitality was an absolute necessity.
Traveling evangelists like Paul did not have a variety of
motels to choose from so they were dependent on people
giving them a home away from home. In addition, many new
believers were disowned by their families and were literally
homeless. The young churches accepted responsibility for
them. Times have changed, but many missionary families still

need housing and transport when they are on furlough. And many young women need a loving home as they struggle through an unwanted pregnancy. Loving hospitality is still needed desperately, and those who extend it benefit greatly as well as those who receive it.

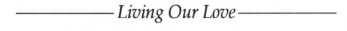

## *Living Our Love*

Set some goals for practicing hospitality.

# Love imitates God

> Be imitators of God, therefore, as dearly loved
> children and live a life of love, just as Christ loved
> us and gave himself up for us as a fragrant offering
> and sacrifice to God. —*Ephesians 5:1-2*

Suppose you've come to the point where you understand the love of God—you've seen God's perfect love and you've seen the way the world around us perverts love. Now you want to commit yourself to love God, to love your neighbor, and to know what it means for the church of God really to demonstrate love.

The above Scripture gives us a command to help us toward that goal. The literal meaning of "dearly loved children" is "as beloved ones." I believe a good father tends to produce children who want to imitate him in certain ways. Very often, the family likeness becomes visible as the children appreciate the good things that are going on in the family and really want to possess those same qualities. As you understand God's love for you, you begin to desire to please him out of your love for him.

Some people respond to a situation in a certain way because they *have* to—there's no way out of it. Others respond because they *want* to. God has made it possible for us to know his love for us. And that knowledge makes the Christian want to do what God wills—to be an imitator. He wants the love of God to flow through his life for no other reason than that he is a beloved one of God. The two things go together. If you know how much God loves you and you respond to his love, you will want to imitate him in his love.

If we are holding to the faith of our Lord Jesus Christ, who is the expression of God, then Jesus becomes our standard. He is the One whose example we seek to emulate. He's our Lord and Savior and Christ—and our example. We look to him for attitudes and for actions.

As we imitate God, we will learn to abstain from those things that do not reflect God's character. As we love and imitate God, as we grow more and more into the character of Christ, our actions will change. Our tastes and longings will change, too, over time. But it starts with obedience: "Be imitators of God . . ."

Our children imitate us without either them or us realizing it. They observe and emulate, sometimes to our embarrassment. But as time goes on they choose their own heroes or models: sometimes they choose wisely, and sometimes they don't. We will in a sense "naturally" begin to reflect the love of God, but we also need the discipline of choosing the right models.

 *Living Our Love*

In what areas of your life do you least reflect God's character? Study the Bible to find out how you can imitate God in these areas.

# Love sacrifices

He who did not spare his own Son, but gave him up
for us all—how will he not also, along with him,
graciously give us all things?          —*Romans 8:32*

There is a strong "sacrificial" aspect to love as we see it in
Scripture. Much of what passes for love today is sentimental
and superficial. By comparison, real love is primarily interested in *giving*—and immaturity is primarily interested in
*getting*. The sacrifice of the Son forms a graphic illustration of
love's perfection. We see that the love of Jesus Christ was such
that he gave himself for us.

There are many, many examples in Scripture of self-
sacrificing love. Love is seen by action, and it is the cost, not
the size of the gift (the widow's mite, the drink of water), that
God sees and encourages.

Love "agape style" is really an act of self-sacrifice, stem-
ming from decision and commitment. A young man once
wrote a letter to his girlfriend: "I love you and I'll climb the
highest mountain, I'll swim the deepest sea, to be with you,
etc." Then he added a P.S.: "And I'll see you on Friday if it isn't
raining." If the depth of his love was measured by what he
was willing to do, the young lady may have been well-advised
to do something else on Friday—rain or shine!

We can measure the love of God by the cost of his gift. Some
think that if they give a lot of money in the offering, this shows
their love for God. The Pharisees thought that the amount of
their money gifts would show others and God how devoted
they were. But it's not always the amount of your dollars—
although sometimes it is. There are many people whom God
has entrusted with wealth, and I'm sure he does consider the
size of their gifts. But it's what the gift costs the giver that

really matters. Remember the widow's mite? In size, it was a tiny gift. In cost, it was an enormous gift. Her gift cost her everything she had. That tiny gift made news in heaven, as far as God was concerned, because it was an act of love.

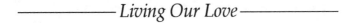

## Living Our Love

What love sacrifices have been made for you by others? Take some moments to thank God for his ultimate sacrifice and for those people who have loved you through sacrifice.

# Love leads to real forgiveness

> Get rid of all bitterness, rage and anger, brawling and slander, along with every form of malice. Be kind and compassionate to one another, forgiving each other, just as in Christ God forgave you.
>
> —*Ephesians 4:31-32*

Very often we pray as if God owes us something, as if we are deserving of special treatment. The question is often asked, "Why do bad things happen to good people?" The unspoken assumption being, apparently, that God should give us more good stuff and exempt us from the bad. God indicates that if we get what we deserve we'll be in a fine mess. And if he gives us what we've really earned, we'll be in an even bigger mess. But he is prepared to deal with us not on the basis of what we've earned or deserved, but on the basis of love and grace. His love is such that he is prepared to forgive us and to give us the gift of pardon, which we could not have merited under any circumstances. Our great difficulty with understanding the concept of pardon and forgiveness as opposed to grace and mercy shows how limited our understanding of God's love truly is, and how exaggerated is our view of our own goodness.

We need a clearer understanding of the forgiveness of the Father. We subconsciously seem to think that there is something in us that merits divine favor. Very often we have a sneaking suspicion that God did the right thing when he gave us the gift of his grace because, really, if there ever was a deserving case, it was you and me. The Scriptures teach that God gave us what he gave us for no other reason than that he is a loving God. We must come to terms with that in order to be the humble, repentant people that God requires us to be.

The perfection of love is seen completely in the forgiveness of God the Father. The Greek word for forgiveness is *charizomai*, related to *charis*, which means "grace." The idea of forgiveness is that it is a gift of grace, something that is totally undeserved and utterly unmerited.

Yet when we set out to forgive others, we often require that they earn or deserve it. They must feel sorry enough, and say it in just the right way. They must admit in what ways they were wrong (and often we want that phrased just so, too). And, even after we've said we've forgiven them, inside there is a reserve toward them, in case they offend us again. If anything we become more sensitive to possible offenses than ever before. And if they are unfortunate enough to make *another* error, then we swoop down on it like a bird of prey waiting for that little field mouse to show up. This is not the "forgiveness" into which love leads us. Remember that love learns to expect the best from people, to give them the benefit of the doubt. God certainly gives us the benefit of the doubt; this is the least we can do for one another.

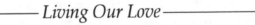 *Living Our Love*

Ask the Holy Spirit to search your heart and show you where your forgiveness is not in character with God's forgiveness.

# Love can handle interruptions

> So they went away by themselves in a boat to a
> solitary place. But many who saw them leaving
> recognized them and ran on foot from all the towns
> and got there ahead of them. When Jesus landed
> and saw a large crowd, he had compassion on
> them, because they were like sheep without a
> shepherd. So he began teaching them many things.
> —*Mark 6:32-34*

We all remember the incident when Jesus fed five thousand. But we tend to forget that he really wanted some rest, but found he needed to take care of thousands of hungry souls. He and his disciples rowed all the way across the lake to get away from the crowd. But when they arrived at the other side, they were waiting for him. They'd run around the lake to meet Jesus (not a small accomplishment). So Jesus forgot about his own need for solitude, and an incredible miracle took place.

Did you ever get interrupted by the multitude? As you work, minister, mark off your tasks and errands for the day, try to get to that project that's been waiting forever—do you ever have to deal with a multitude? Who intrudes into your schedule? Perhaps you are a young mother; in that case you have a little multitude around to provide plenty of interruptions. My little multitude is named Peter. He's a big multitude now, all six feet and six inches of him, but for years he was my little multitude. I had to remember the lesson Jesus taught me when he lovingly attended to the multitude or needs that met him instead of his own.

I've learned through the example of my husband in this aspect of love. Stuart has prepared for thousands of spiritual lectures, and he has never prepared behind closed doors. He said at the beginning of our marriage: "The door to my study [although for years he never had a study!] must always be open. I don't want the children feeling they're shut out. And they can come in whenever they wish and ask me a question or interrupt me. It's very important." I've truly been impressed by that. And I've also been irritated on his behalf as I've seen them walking in and out, interrupting important business he's had to do. But I've never seen him lose his temper. And you know, that's how it's got to be. Love enables you to be interrupted by the multitude and not get irritated. That happens when you're more interested in the other person than you are about yourself.

If we get angry at our kids when they interrupt us, they will interpret that as a lack of love. What's the point of saying we love them, cuddling and kissing them one moment, then blowing up at them awhile later when they interrupt something we're doing? Keep in mind that the word "children" doesn't necessarily mean your biological children. We have spiritual children, too, some of them having grown up damaged and needing more care, patience, and tenderness than ever. Baby Christians especially seem to go through a crisis a minute—they need to feel that they can depend on someone who will treat them as if they are the only thing on today's agenda. It's possible to do that. And I learned years ago that I can do a great many things and still be present for someone who needs to interrupt. They can bare their soul while I do the ironing; we can talk or pray together in the car as we do errands. Interruptions don't deter love; they merely spur love on to greater resourcefulness and creativity.

———————— *Living Our Love* ————————

When are you most likely to feel interrupted? How can you prepare to approach this situation differently?

# Love overrules self-importance

> Do nothing out of selfish ambition or vain conceit,
> but in humility consider others better than
> yourselves. Each of you should look not only to
> your own interests, but also to the interests of others.
> —*Philippians 2:3-4*

If I love, if I am primarily interested in the well-being of the people I teach, then I can teach even the hard things in love. And those who listen will know that love is my motive. If the gift is used in love, people will be changed. Paul said that unloving people "though [they] understand all mysteries and all knowledge" are ineffective in serving people. Some people are very intelligent; some have tremendous spiritual knowledge. They've got biblical knowledge coming out of their ears; they exude spiritual wisdom. But without the control of love, the most gifted people may become conceited, big-headed— "sounding brass or tinkling cymbals"!

J. B. Phillips translated 1 Corinthians 1:8: "We should remember that while knowledge may make a man look big, it's only love that can make him grow to his full stature. For whatever a man may know, he still has a lot to learn." Sometimes I hear people say, "The Lord told me this," as if God hadn't said anything to anyone else. They affect some extra quality of spirituality and speak as if their special insight is not only the last word, but the only word. No doubt God has taught them something, but their approach sometimes rubs you the wrong way. In a way, they suggest that God is only talking to them!

Somehow when the Spirit of God does speak through someone there is a ring of truth about it. For example, when William Carey, "the father of modern missions," presented his concern for the unreached people of the day to a group of ministers he was told, "Young man, sit down. When God pleases to convert the heathen, he will do it without your aid or mine." Carey sat down, but he didn't give up. We all know about him. But the other man, claiming superior wisdom, has disappeared nameless into the mists of history.

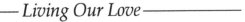

## Living Our Love

What questions do you enjoy being asked about yourself? (Some people like to talk about their children; others want to tell people about their work, their dreams, funny things that have happened to them, their positions on important issues, etc.) The next time you are in conversation with someone, make a point to ask those questions about him or her, turning the focus away from yourself.

# Love transforms

For you were once darkness, but now you are light
in the Lord. Live as children of light (for the fruit of
the light consists in all goodness, righteousness and
truth) and find out what pleases the Lord.

—*Ephesians 5:8-10*

God is not only concerned about getting man into heaven,
but also about getting heaven into man. He manages to do
that when somebody opens up their heart and invites the
Holy Spirit to come in.

Christianity is not just going to church, and it's not just
having your sins forgiven and going to heaven when you die.
Christianity is seeing that old sinful nature dealt with and the
power of the Spirit released and the evidence of it in fruit,
which firstly is love.

The Spirit isn't self-absorbed. He speaks of Christ. So if I
have within me the Holy Spirit and what he says I say and
what he thinks I think, then it follows that what he is, I
become, to the extent that my old self-centered sinful nature
is controlled by him. The Spirit of God empowers me to live
the life of love so that my thoughts, affections, speech, purposes, and actions are under his control, the control of love.

This takes place as we get into God's Word, and it begins
to change us. And as we decide before him what we do, what
we say, what we speak, and try in obedience to do what we
find in this book, then he steps behind us, helping us. We
begin the obedience, and God is there to help us finish it. We
have to open our mouth to speak in love. We have to stretch
out our hands and do the action. And as we do, we find the
power available to us.

At the end of World War II God raised up a man, an Englishman, called Major Ian Thomas, who had a special love for young people. He had been in Germany and seen the lives of young people molded by Nazism. And God laid upon him a love for those young men. He made arrangements for many of them to come to England where they heard the gospel and saw it in action. Many of them were won for Jesus Christ. Now they're scattered all around the world because God's Spirit remolded them from within. They became pastors and teachers and missionaries. Two of them bravely gave their lives on the East German border, seeking to help Christians as the Berlin Wall went up. God's love, in the power of the Holy Spirit, infuses our lives with the power to transform us. What a liberation!

## *Living Our Love*

What needs real transformation in your life? Make this area a focus of prayer this week.

# Love leads us into good works

> For we are God's workmanship, created in Christ
> Jesus to do good works, which God prepared in
> advance for us to do. —*Ephesians 2:10*

God has made us what we are, creating us in Christ Jesus for good deeds. We're not saved *by* good works but to be given, by God, good works to do. Works are not the means of salvation, but they are evidence of it. And as we see that Christ has died for us and risen again so that he might live in us, the gratitude we have for his love toward us should result in service.

Please notice that God has saved us to do "good" works, not "great" works. Some people make a mistake here. They think *Oh, now I'm a Christian. God has saved me to do a great work, to be a Billy Graham or to do something high profile.* Good works may be great, but not all great works are good.

And notice, too, that God has not saved us to be *successful*; we are saved to be *faithful.* In this modern Western culture, we can't imagine anything being good unless it's a great success. We are nurtured toward success, toward greatness. But we see that, in many cases, the people in the Bible who were faithful were not considered successful by their peers, nor would they be by our standards today.

Maybe the good work God has saved you for is caring for an aged parent. Or maybe the good work God has saved you for is caring for two kids with no one but God and a couple of angels looking on. That's possibly the good work that God has saved you for. The attitude with which we approach that to which God has called us and for which he saves us should be one of love for him and whatever he wants us to do.

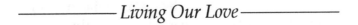

## *Living Our Love*

Think of the Christians you know. What good works have been the result of God's love in their lives? What good works might God's love be leading you into?

# Love learns God's kind of thinking

> Do not conform any longer to the pattern of this
> world, but be transformed by the renewing of your
> mind. Then you will be able to test and approve
> what God's will is—his good, pleasing and perfect
> will.
> —*Romans 12:2*

Paul says in Colossians that we have the mind of Christ
within us. And if his mind is controlling our mind, we can
think God's thoughts after him. Now that sounds like the
most unbelievably arrogant thing someone could ever say.
But I don't know any other way to think right. If I can't think
as Christ thinks—if he can't take my mind and make my mind
his own and think his thoughts through my mind—I'm lost,
because I know what my thoughts are like. Scriptures say
that we are actually partakers of the divine nature if we
know Christ.

We have a choice—either to have a mind that is transformed or a mind that is conformed. If you have a transformed mind, you'll be a spiritual person; yours will be a
mind that learns to understand the things of God. Sadly, it's
much easier to conform to the way the rest of the world thinks.

Whether our minds become transformed or not depends
on what we're feeding them. If we take in the attitudes, the
philosophies, the spiritual approaches of the world around
us, that's the kind of mind we'll have. If we are taking in
God's Word, feeding on the attitudes and approaches that
spring from prayer and Bible study and participation with
other growing Christians, the transformation of our minds
can take place.

As the Holy Spirit makes us sensitive to sin, as we begin to
think thoughts that are very different from the thoughts

around us, we begin to think differently about everything. Think about the messages prime-time television gives us about marriage, divorce, and sexuality—pretty sad, aren't they? But if that's all you're taking in, you won't hear the Holy Spirit over the television set. As we listen to the Holy Spirit, however, those television signals grow weaker and weaker. We begin to see through the confusion and delusions of the world. We're able to see sin for what it is, and we can take a better way—all because our minds have been transformed.

Love begins to think right. And when love thinks right, it thinks no evil. You see, love doesn't say, "Every man for himself." Love doesn't say, "I'm going to get revenge." Love is not puffed up, saying, "I've got rights." Love doesn't say, "I don't care what you think." But our culture does.

Which path will you choose—God's, or the world's?

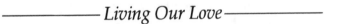 *Living Our Love*

Is there any way in which you are taking in too much of the world's mind? How can you remedy that? What steps can you take to allow the Holy Spirit to transform your mind?

# Taking love to the pub

[The master of the banquet said] "Go out quickly
into the streets and alleys of the town and bring in
the poor, the crippled, the blind and the lame."
"Sir," the servant said, "what you ordered has been
done, but there is still room." Then the master told
his servant, "Go out to the roads and country lanes
and make them come in, so that my house will be
full."

—*from Jesus' parable of the wedding banquet, Luke 14:15-24*

In the days when Stuart was traveling the world preaching,
I decided that something had to be done about the neighborhood. So I got a list of all the drinking places nearby and a
bunch of us set out to go into them to sing some hymns around
the bar piano and to speak to the customers. We were not
refused once at any of the thirty-five pubs we visited. Why?
Because the pub owners held the view of Christianity that it
was powerless and couldn't change anything anyway. If
they'd really understood the kind of life changes we were
after, they wouldn't have let us in. We could have closed
their business!

Bibles in hand, we'd come into a bar full of drinking people,
and everyone would turn around to look at us. I'd announce,
"Hello, everybody. We've just come in to talk with you and
visit. We thought we might have a hymn sing tonight." There
was always a sort of shocked silence. Then someone would
say, "Come on, then, Love." And they loved it. They would
get us settled at the piano and start requesting their favorite
hymns. They would actually sing along with old hymns.
Sometimes tears would run down their faces. The old favor-
ites really brought back memories for some of those people.

We had a tremendous time as we sat with them and talked about the Lord. But it saddened me that as soon as they saw the Bibles and heard our announcement of who we were and where we'd come from, every hand would go to their pocket. Immediately, they thought, *Here is the church, coming begging.* How sad that this was their picture of the church, of Christianity—a few hymns and then a passing of the plate—especially when love involves so much more (conversation, accepting people where they are, being willing to sit in a smoke-filled, liquor-filled environment and actually feel the hurts and needs there). We can't expect many of these people to go out to the church, looking for love. No, love must seek out those people who need to know its reality. Love goes looking.

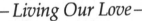

## Living Our Love

Going to a drinking establishment may not be the most effective way to take God's love to people in the United States; many such places are too noisy with blaring music to even have conversations. And in a lot of them, "soliciting" includes evangelism and isn't allowed by the proprietors. But the principle can be applied. We need to take the love of Jesus to where the people are and not expect them to come to us. What are some ways you can take love to the people who need it?

# Love brings repentance

Godly sorrow brings repentance that leads to
salvation and leaves no regret, but worldly sorrow
brings death.
                                    —*2 Corinthians 7:10*

The goodness of God is meant to lead us to repentance. I
remember sitting in a little room at Cambridge University. I
had come to faith in Christ while lying in a hospital bed. Now
I was better, back at school trying to pick up the threads of
college life again. One afternoon my advising professor allowed me to use her sitting room. "Jill, why don't you put on
a fire and sit here and read awhile. I know what it's like down
in the dorm."

I took the opportunity and read a booklet called *Christian
Certainty* by Frederick P. Wood that explained the love of God
and what he had done for me. And it was there in my
professor's room that my heart was broken as I read about
Christ's dying for me, as if there were no one else in the world.
I cried and cried. The goodness of God led me to true repentance. The Holy Spirit, having come into my heart, explained
to me from within how much God loved me. I loved him at
that moment because, and only because, he first loved me. I
saw his love, that he had not withheld his only Son. I have
two sons now, and I wouldn't give up either of them. Yet God
gave his only Son—while I was still a sinner—that I might
be forgiven.

One day my teenage daughter called on the phone. She was
baby-sitting in a friend's home. "Mom," she said, "I'm calling
to say I'm sorry for being such a little snot." I was surprised
to hear her say that, so I asked her, "Why have you called to
say you're sorry this evening?" She replied, "When the kids
were asleep I started to think about you and how kind you've

been to me. Even when I've been difficult you've kept on loving me. I just need to say I'm sorry and I love you." I understood then what Paul meant about the goodness of God leading to repentance.

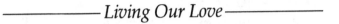

—————————— *Living Our Love* ——————————

When have you been sorry, but not repentant for something you said or did? When have you truly been repentant? What difference did repentance make in your life?

# Seeing others through divine eyes

> Jesus went through all the towns and villages,
> teaching in their synagogues, preaching the good
> news of the kingdom and healing every disease and
> sickness. When he saw the crowds, he had
> compassion on them, because they were harassed
> and helpless, like sheep without a shepherd.
>
> —*Matthew 9:35-36*

Paul says in one passage, "So from now on, we regard no one from a worldly point of view" (2 Corinthians 5:16). Paul means that if the love of God touches us, our love for him will mean that we'll live for him rather than for ourselves. We'll begin to look at people through divine spectacles. Love learns to put itself in the other person's place and understand what he or she is going through. In this Scripture from Matthew, we see Jesus looking out over a crowd of selfish, miserable, sinful, demanding people—and what did he see? Needs. People in need of a shepherd. He had a special perspective, looking through love's eyes.

When we begin to see with love's eyes, we don't see people who must be tolerated, or people we like or dislike. Neither do we see people to be used, to be hired or fired, to fight, or to take advantage of. We've turned our back on the "worldly point of view." What we see now is people who in their deep need are loved by God, for whom Christ died, people who are redeemable, who in all their shame are significant, who in all their weakness have potential for glory. This point of view is utterly life-changing.

And as we develop a tremendous concern for the spiritual well-being of others, we come to recognize our role as Christ's ambassadors; we can introduce others to the Christ who can give them life and care for their needs. As children of God we will develop a vision for broken lives being mended, for fragmented, sinful people becoming whole.

That's what happens when you understand the love of God. The love of God flowing from you changes your attitude toward your own life, your attitude toward people, and the emphasis of your being. Whatever your vocation, occupation, calling, residence, your overriding concern will be not to exacerbate the pain and disruption people already have to contend with, but to throw your energies into being a part of their restoration, not condemnation.

Assuming you've been touched by his love and have become motivated by love, then when you're in the midst of the mess that is our world you're Christ's ambassador and an agent of reconciliation. What a privilege to be a life-changer in your area of influence!

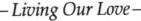
## Living Our Love

We can talk in grandiose terms about calling the church to take the gospel to the world. Take a moment to focus on individuals you know. Ask yourself, *Do I love God because he first loved me, and does it show in my attitudes and my lifestyle? Am I truly an ambassador of Christ? Am I honestly an agent of reconciliation?*

# Love grows up

> When I was a child, I talked like a child, I thought
> like a child, I reasoned like a child. When I became a
> man, I put childish ways behind me.
>
> —*1 Corinthians 13:11*

Here Paul is developing the illustration that all things are incomplete at this present time, but when glory comes everything will be finished. And when it is finished we will see it all in perspective. Paul compares it to being a little kid and thinking and feeling and reasoning and arguing like a little kid, and then growing up. That makes all the difference in the world.

Right now, we are still in the "little kid" stage. One day, "when perfection comes," we'll be grown up. Then we'll look back at these days and laugh at the childish behavior that hurt others. Then we'll totally comprehend—we will understand what God was doing all along! We'll see that, through everything, God was growing us up in him.

Growth doesn't happen overnight, although it sometimes includes critical moments; occasionally we have to make choices for growth and not stagnation. We have to say, "Okay, I'm going to be the spiritual person God wants me to be." Although God gives us the ability to mature spiritually, we participate in the process by making choices and following through. What level of life will we live on? Basic instinct? Reactions rather than decisive actions? Stagnation and "safety" rather than the life full of adventures God has in store? We can grow up into mature, loving creatures as God designed, or we can remain childish. A lot of adults are still quite childish in the way they approach their tasks, their problems, and their relationships. If we choose to stay children, we will have company, but it won't be very stimulating or satisfying.

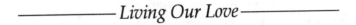 *Living Our Love*

In what areas of your life do you see real growth and development? What contributed to that growth? In what areas are you still reverting to childish patterns, and why? What can you do to remedy these areas of stagnation?

# The restored image

> At one time we too were foolish, disobedient,
> deceived and enslaved by all kinds of passions and
> pleasures . . . We lived in malice and envy, being
> hated and hating one another. But when the
> kindness and love of God our Savior appeared, he
> saved us, not because of righteous things we have
> done, but because of his mercy. He saved us
> through the washing of rebirth and renewal by the
> Holy Spirit, whom he poured out on us generously
> through Jesus Christ our Savior, so that, having
> been justified by his grace, we might become heirs
> having the hope of eternal life.      —*Titus 3:3-7*

He restores my soul" is a familiar phrase from Psalm 23. The word *restored* means that something is made into the image that's been lost. My mother acquired a lot of antiques for her beautiful manor house in England. To me, they were rather ugly lumps of wood. But she used to work on them. I remember her bringing one piece in and I said, "Oh Mother, what on earth is that?" She replied, "It's the most beautiful piece!" and told me all about it. I said that it just looked like an old piece of wood. Her answer: "It's lost its image."

Well, my mother worked and worked on that piece. Eventually the image that had been lost came through. And it was indeed a beautiful piece of furniture. It's one of the precious things we brought with us from England. It stands in our home now, reminding me of a spiritual principle: that it cost my mom almost more to restore it than to buy it.

I think of God and I think of my life—loveless, carnal, selfish, irritable, impatient. And yet I know because I am a human being, different from an animal, that somewhere is the image of God that needs to be restored.

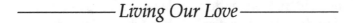

——————— *Living Our Love* ———————

As you read your Bible during the next few days, look for clues about the divine image that God is restoring in you. What will you look and act like eventually, as that image becomes more defined?

# A society of love

> You are the light of the world. A city on a hill cannot
> be hidden. Neither do people light a lamp and put
> it under a bowl. Instead they put it on its stand, and
> it gives light to everyone in the house. In the same
> way, let your light shine before men, that they may
> see your good deeds and praise your Father in
> heaven. —*Matthew 5:14-16*

The church of Christ is God's society placed in the middle of
a fragmented, secular society. Paul teaches what God's society
is meant to be like. The people within God's church are unique
in that they have experienced conversion—that changing
experience that transforms them from what they were into
what God eventually wants them to be. Regeneration begins
when a person comes in repentance and faith to Jesus Christ
and knows forgiveness of sins, and then moves into an ongoing experience in which he or she is continually being changed
into the image of God's Son through the work of the indwell-
ing Holy Spirit.

Jesus gave to us—his followers—the Comforter, the Holy
Spirit, to empower us as individuals and as a society within
society. Who is this Holy Spirit? He isn't an influence. He isn't
a vague eminence. He isn't an ecstatic feeling. He isn't an itch.
He isn't an old English spook that inhabits old English houses.
I was a student at Cambridge when I first heard of "the Holy
Ghost." I knew nothing about the Holy Spirit, but I did know
what a ghost was. So I figured the Holy Ghost must be some
sort of a good ghost. I didn't know it was a term used for a
coequal member of the Trinity. The Holy Spirit is the One who
shapes believers of all types into a body with a shared purpose
and shared energy—the energy and purpose of agape love.

You may or may not have great visions or talents, but you do have God's Word that shines into darkened souls. You do have the Spirit of God who applies that Word to every area of life. And you do have the prayers of God's people. When all these things come together, people's eyes are opened. We joke about people "seeing the light," but it's quite accurate. Some people, like Saul of Tarsus, walk along the road of their lives absolutely convinced that they're doing great and that Jesus, at best, is irrelevant. Then they see the light, discovering that they are far from doing great. They see themselves as totally unsatisfactory in the divine eyes and realize that Christ is their only hope.

How do they see this? Where does the light come from? From the love of God demonstrated in the society of Christians—the church. When people walk through a very unloving world and suddenly stumble upon a group of people who are oddly but wonderfully different in the way they treat one another, that's bright enough to open even a cynic's eyes!

There's a lot of animosity in secular society when it comes to the formal church, that is, the various institutions that come under the title of "the church." Sometimes "the church" isn't much of a light at all. But when the Holy Spirit moves among Christians, and they love with God's agape love, even a hostile surrounding society will see the light in front of it— that, or put blinders on and go on its way.

## Living Our Love

When and how did you first see God's "light"? In what ways do you think *you* are a light to others? (If you have trouble with this question, ask some honest people who know you—you'll be surprised at the light God can bring out in your life, even when you are unaware of it showing.)

# Love makes the difference

> If I speak in the tongues of men and angels, but
> have not love, I am only a resounding gong or a
> clanging cymbal. If I have the gift of prophecy and
> can fathom all mysteries and all knowledge, and if I
> have a faith that can move mountains, but have not
> love, I am nothing. —*1 Corinthians 13:1-2*

In the book of 1 Corinthians Paul deals with people who are tremendously gifted but are not living out love. This situation is what prompted him to describe love in detail in chapter 13. He needed to spell out to them what love is—and what, frankly, they were not.

If we really concentrate on these first few verses of 1 Corinthians 13, we can't help but become nervous because we see that it is possible to believe in God, to love his Son, to have come to a knowledge of Christ as Savior—and just to be making a lot of noise.

The Scriptures describe Jesus in the first chapter of John's gospel as being "full of grace and truth." Well, we can be full of grace but very little truth: this leads to cults and very zealous but very wrong Christians. And sometimes we've got truth, but no grace to temper it. We all know people who are very knowledgeable about the Bible but who are lacking in love. This is what Paul is talking about. We can know all there is to know, even have miraculous faith, but in the end it is *love* that makes the difference in the lives of ourselves and others.

There's nothing so hard and unyielding as somebody who knows a lot of truth but is not tempered by agape love. Sometimes in marriage counseling therapists ask questions like, "Which is more important, to be right or to be at peace with your partner?" To some people, being right is of ultimate importance. And that applies to their faith lives as well. But God says, "Here's the best thing of all—love. Love like the love I've shown you."

However gifted you are, in whatever area your gift is, there's not room for having a big head about it. And it's just not appropriate for a Christian to run around making a lot of noise about his or her gifts, faith, or knowledge. If somebody knows you don't love them, they're not going to listen to what you say, anyway. But if they know that you love them and you have shown them that you love them, your love will make inroads into their lives.

If you notice people putting hands over their ears when you try to communicate with them, maybe that's because they are hearing the noise but not sensing the love.

## Living Our Love

How do people know that you love them? What actions and words could they point to in order to be sure it's love and not something else?

# The girl and the bell tower

"My command is this: Love each other as I have loved. Greater love has no one than this, that he lay down his life for his friends." —*John 15:12-13*

This is a true story, taken down by a poet who was present at the event. There was a young couple in Cromwell's time. The young man was a soldier. Evidently he did something wrong, and Cromwell condemned him to death. Cromwell said that when the curfew bell rang, the young soldier would be put to death. And so the people gathered in the village square as they did in those days, to hang him.

The young wife of this soldier knew that when the curfew bell—the huge bell in the tower—rang, her beloved would die. So she climbed up the tower and hung onto the clapper of the bell. When it was time, the old sexton who had rung the bell all his life began to pull the rope. The young girl was smashed against the side of the bell again and again and again. And everybody stood in the square, waiting for the execution of the soldier.

Finally, the puzzled sexton finished trying to ring the bell. Cromwell asked him why the bell had not been rung. And the young girl climbed down, bleeding and bruised, and told Cromwell what she had done:

> At his feet she told her story,
> Showed her hands all bruised and torn
> And her sweet young face filled with anguish.
> Cromwell's heart was touched with pity,
> Wet his eyes with misty light.
> "Girl, your love will live this evening,
> Curfew will not ring tonight."

Love gives itself. Love has a redemptive quality. And if we love, then we're willing even to die for those that we love.

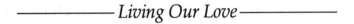
## *Living Our Love*

We need to pray for those who are suffering for their faith—who are condemned to death not by Cromwell, but by those antagonists to Christianity. We need each other in a world where Christians are persecuted for their faith. Who can you pray for today?

# Prayer

Gracious Lord, of all the challenging words concerning our own behavior, it's doubtful that any are more challenging than: "A new commandment I give you, that you love one another." Nothing is more challenging than to be told to love God with all our heart, and all our soul, and all our strength, our neighbor as ourselves, and then to love our enemies.

What decisions we have to make! What needs we have in this area. We humbly bow before you—not in despair, but to say, "God, if the fruit of the Spirit is love, and the evidence that our old nature is being dealt with and the new nature is being released is to be seen in the fruit of the Spirit, then in dependence on you and in obedience to your Word, I'll move out in obedience and faith and learn what it means to love. Thank you for hearing this prayer. Amen."